Looking west over Streatley Warren

AF215349

THE RIDGEWAY NATIONAL TRAIL

The Ridgeway National Trail runs from Overton Hill near Avebury in Wiltshire to Ivinghoe Beacon in Buckinghamshire, taking in world-famous archaeological sites and two National Landscapes. Suitable for walkers and trekkers at all levels of experience, the 86 mile (139km) waymarked route can be comfortably completed in a week.

Contents and using this guide

This booklet of Ordnance Survey® 1:25,000 Explorer® maps has been designed for convenient use on the trail and includes:

- a key to map pages (pages 2–3) showing where to find the maps for each stage
- the full and up-to-date line of the National Trail, designed for use westbound or eastbound and including an extension to historic Avebury
- detours to sites of interest and villages where facilities may be found
- an extract from the OS Explorer map legend (pages 56–58).

In addition, the *The Ridgeway National Trail* guidebook describes the full route in both directions with lots of other practical and historical information.

© Cicerone Press 2026

Second edition 2026

ISBN-13: 978 1 78631 292 1

First edition 2016

Photos © Steve Davison

MIX
Paper | Supporting
responsible forestry
FSC® C010256

© Crown copyright and database rights 2026 OS AC0000810376

Printed in China on responsibly sourced paper on behalf of Latitude Press Ltd.

Cicerone's EU representative for GPSR compliance is Easy Access System Europe, Mustamäe tee 50, 10621 Tallinn, Estonia. Email gpsr.requests@easproject.com.

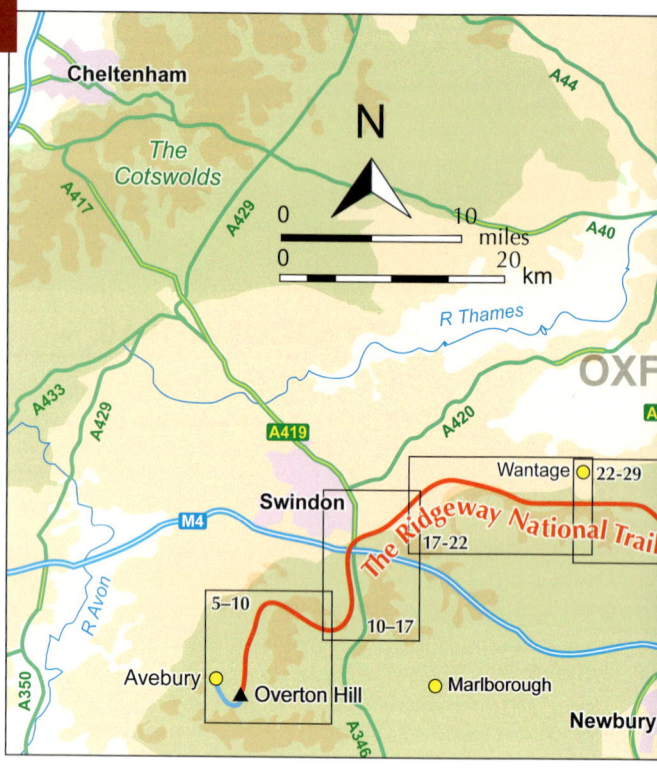

THE RIDGEWAY NATIONAL TRAIL

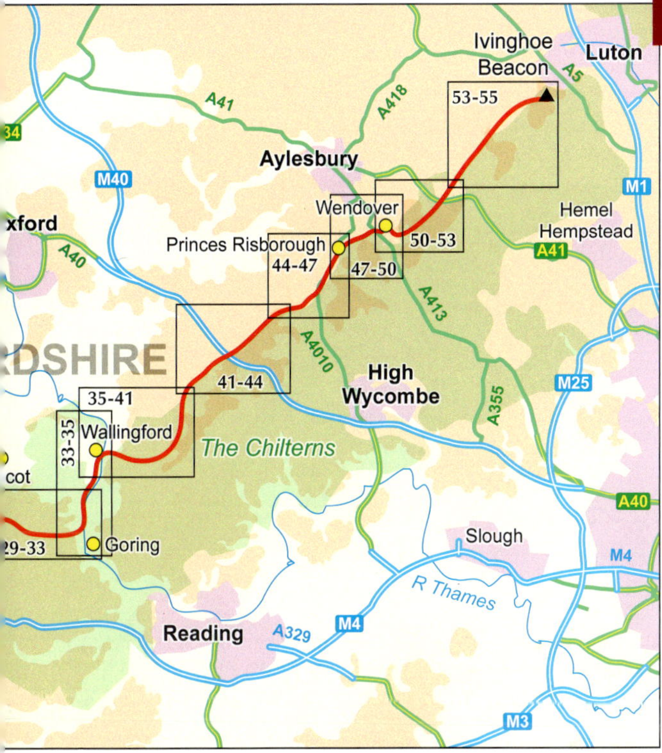

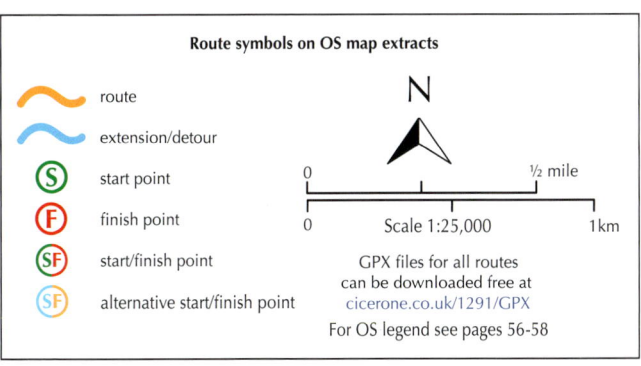

Ivinghoe
Beacon
Luton

A5

53-55

A41
A418

M40
M1

Aylesbury

Wendover

xford
Princes Risborough
50-53
Hemel
Hempstead
A40
44-47
A41

47-50

A413

A4010
High
Wycombe

RDSHIRE
A355
M25

35-41
41-44

33-35
Wallingford
The Chilterns
A40

cot
M4

29-33
Goring
Slough

R Thames

Reading
A329
M4

M3

Route symbols on OS map extracts

~~~ route

~~~ extension/detour

(S) start point

N

(F) finish point

0   ½ mile

(SF) start/finish point

0   1km
Scale 1:25,000

(SF) alternative start/finish point

GPX files for all routes
can be downloaded free at
cicerone.co.uk/1291/GPX

For OS legend see pages 56-58

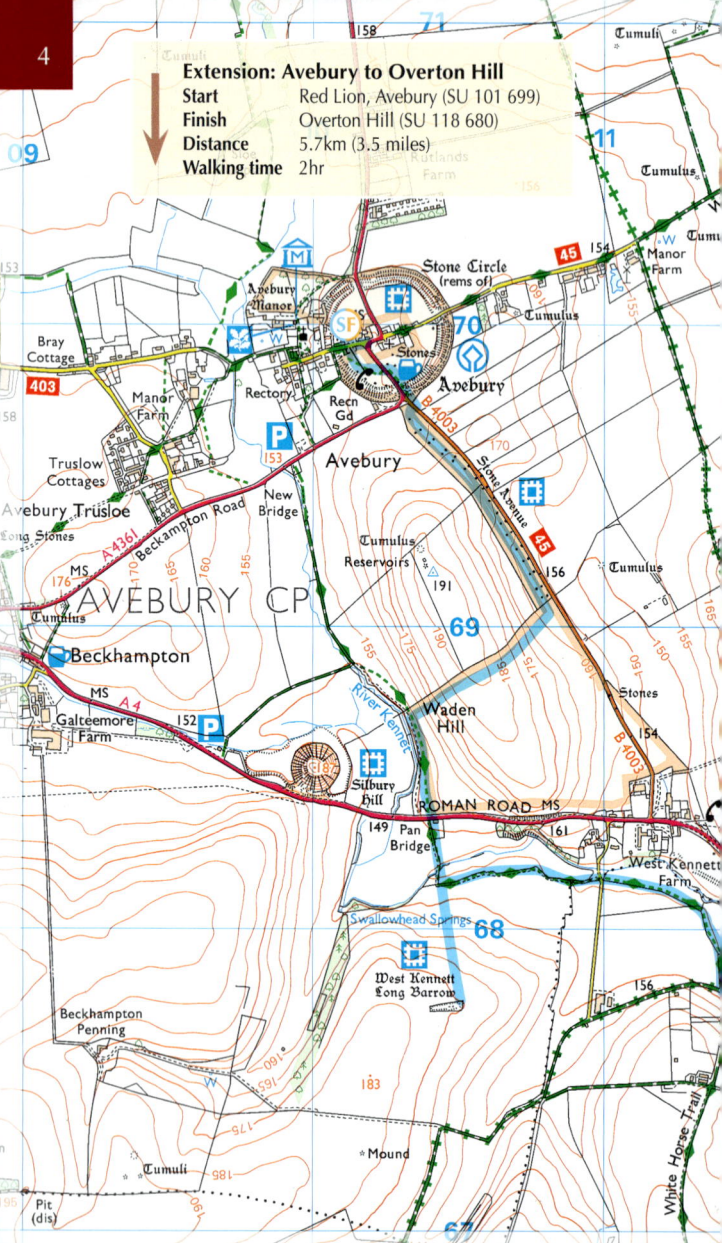

Extension: Avebury to Overton Hill

Start	Red Lion, Avebury (SU 101 699)
Finish	Overton Hill (SU 118 680)
Distance	5.7km (3.5 miles)
Walking time	2hr

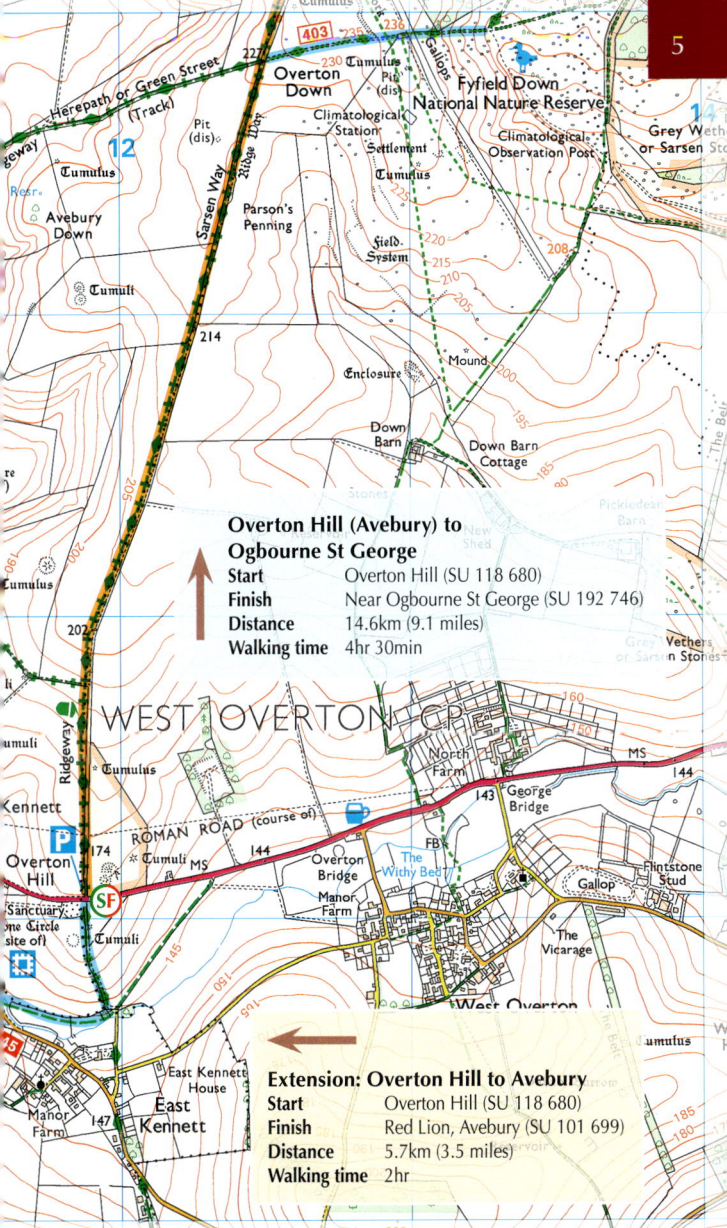

Overton Hill (Avebury) to Ogbourne St George

Start	Overton Hill (SU 118 680)
Finish	Near Ogbourne St George (SU 192 746)
Distance	14.6km (9.1 miles)
Walking time	4hr 30min

Extension: Overton Hill to Avebury

Start	Overton Hill (SU 118 680)
Finish	Red Lion, Avebury (SU 101 699)
Distance	5.7km (3.5 miles)
Walking time	2hr

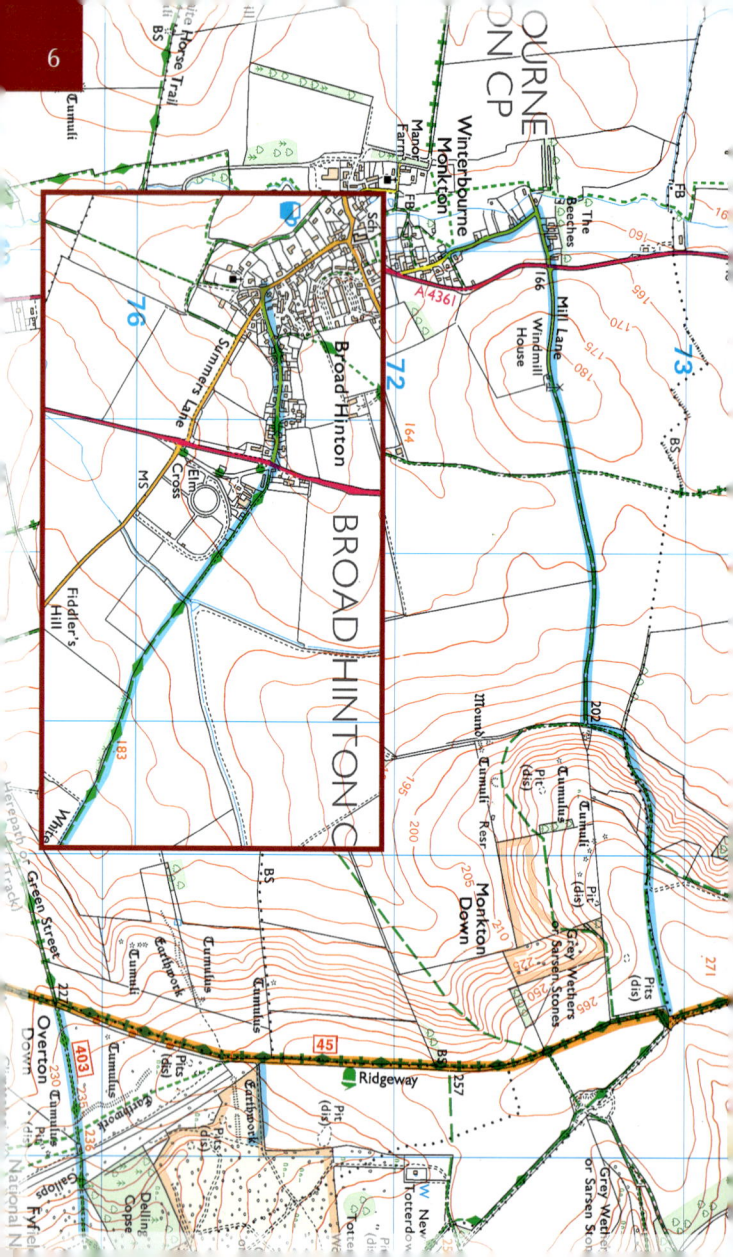

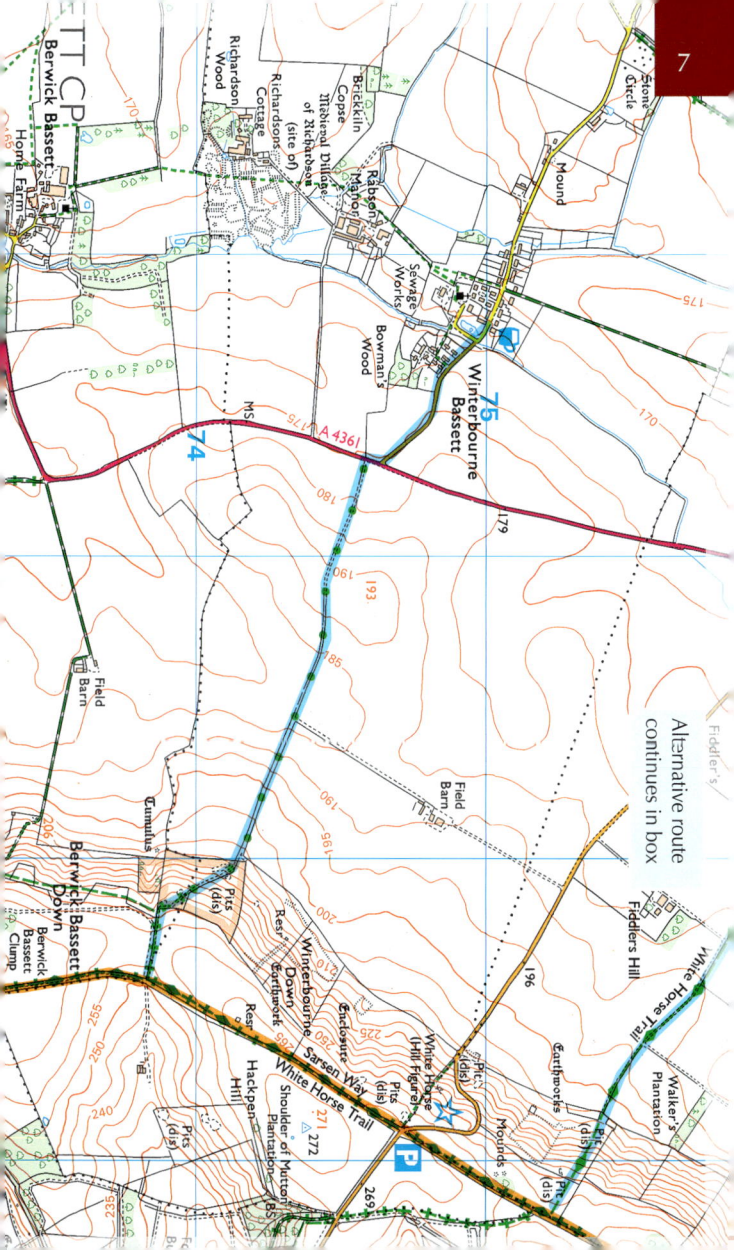

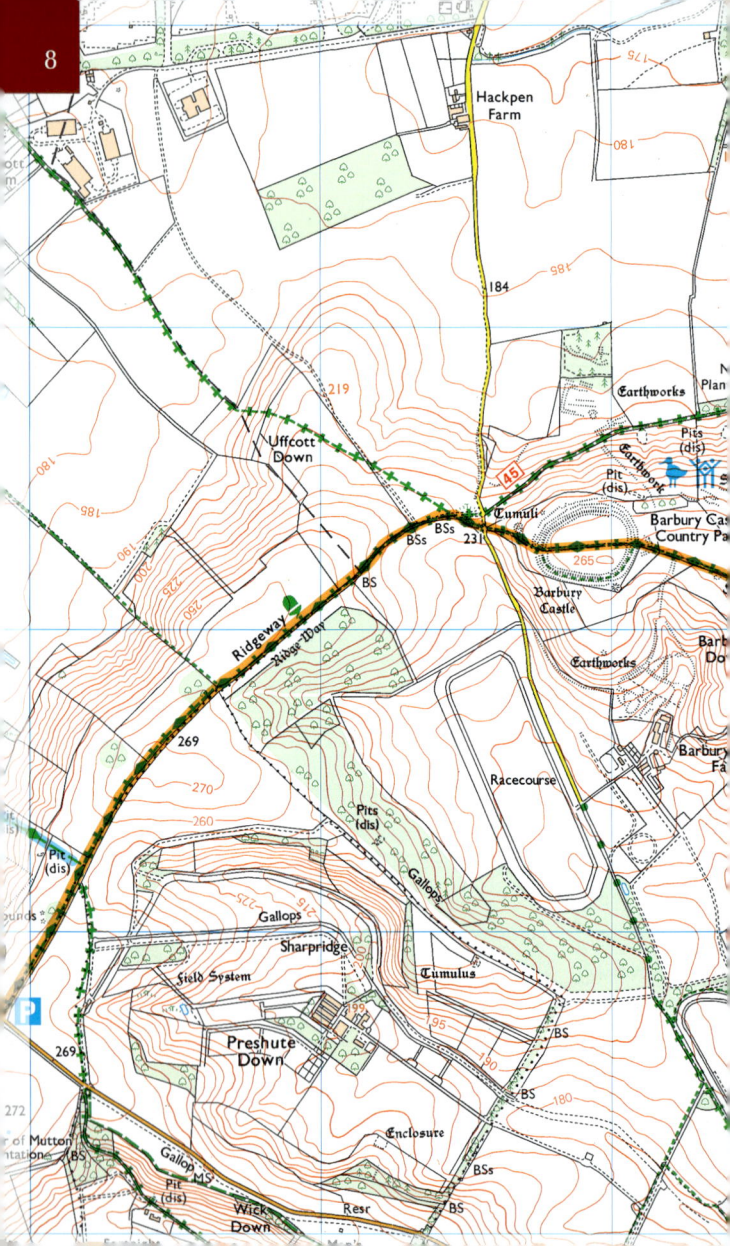

Hackpen
Farm

184

Earthworks

Pits
(dis)

Pit
(dis)

Tumuli

Uffcott
Down

Barbury Ca
Country Pa

BSs
BSs
231

Barbury
Castle

Earthworks

Bart
Do

BS

Ridgeway

Ridge Way

269

Barbury
Fa

270

Racecourse

260

Pits
(dis)

Pit
(dis)

Gallops

Gallops

Sharpridge

Tumulus

Field System

BS

Preshute
Down

195

180

269

BS

272

r of Mutton
ntation

Gallops MS

Pit
(dis)

Enclosure

BS

BSs

Resr

BS

Wick
Down

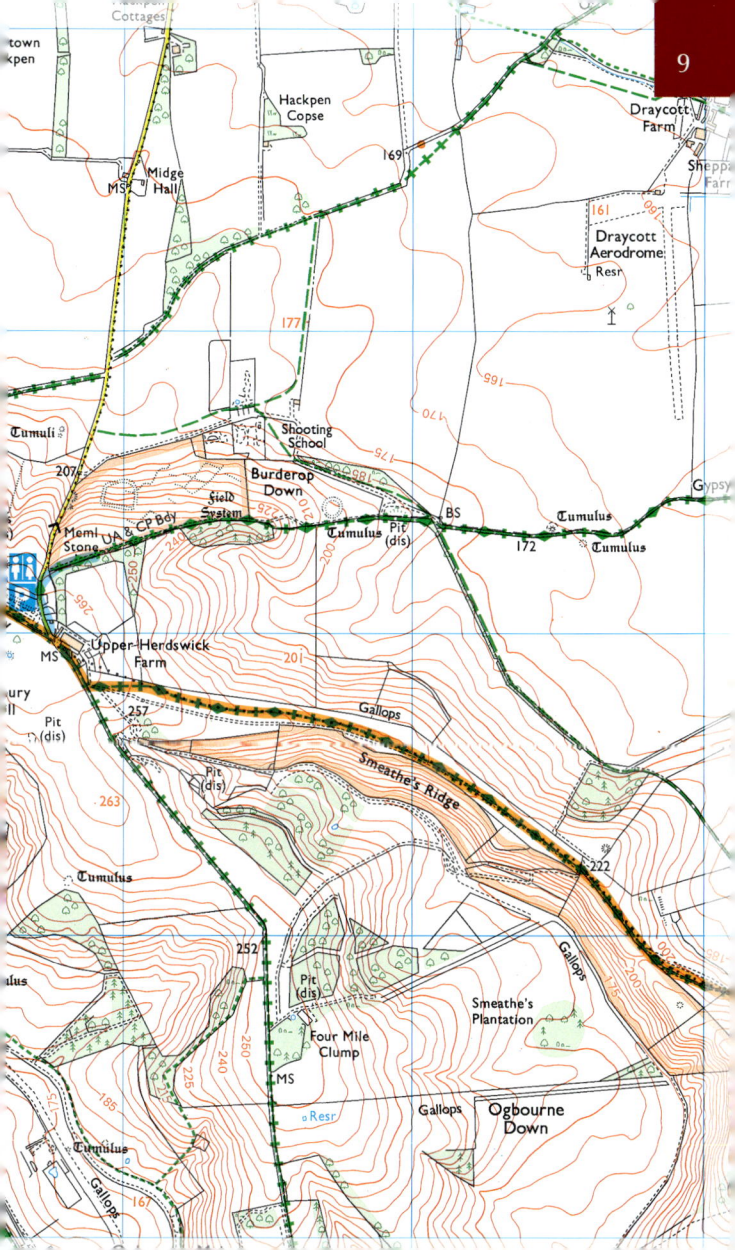

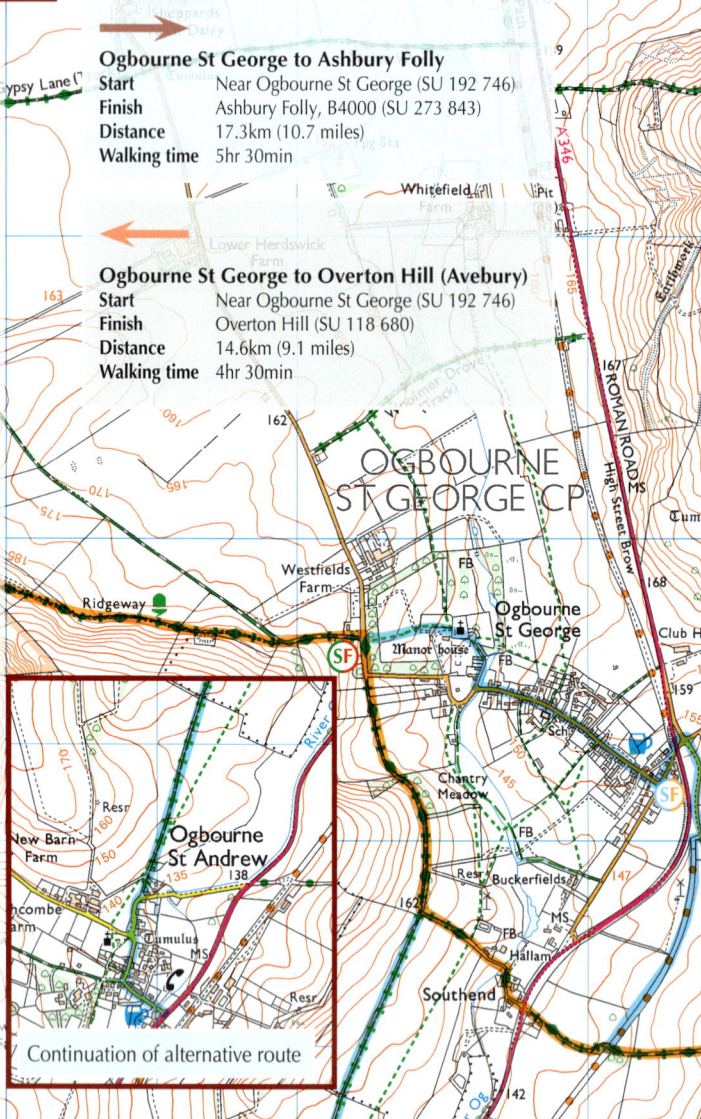

Ogbourne St George to Ashbury Folly

Start	Near Ogbourne St George (SU 192 746)
Finish	Ashbury Folly, B4000 (SU 273 843)
Distance	17.3km (10.7 miles)
Walking time	5hr 30min

Ogbourne St George to Overton Hill (Avebury)

Start	Near Ogbourne St George (SU 192 746)
Finish	Overton Hill (SU 118 680)
Distance	14.6km (9.1 miles)
Walking time	4hr 30min

Continuation of alternative route

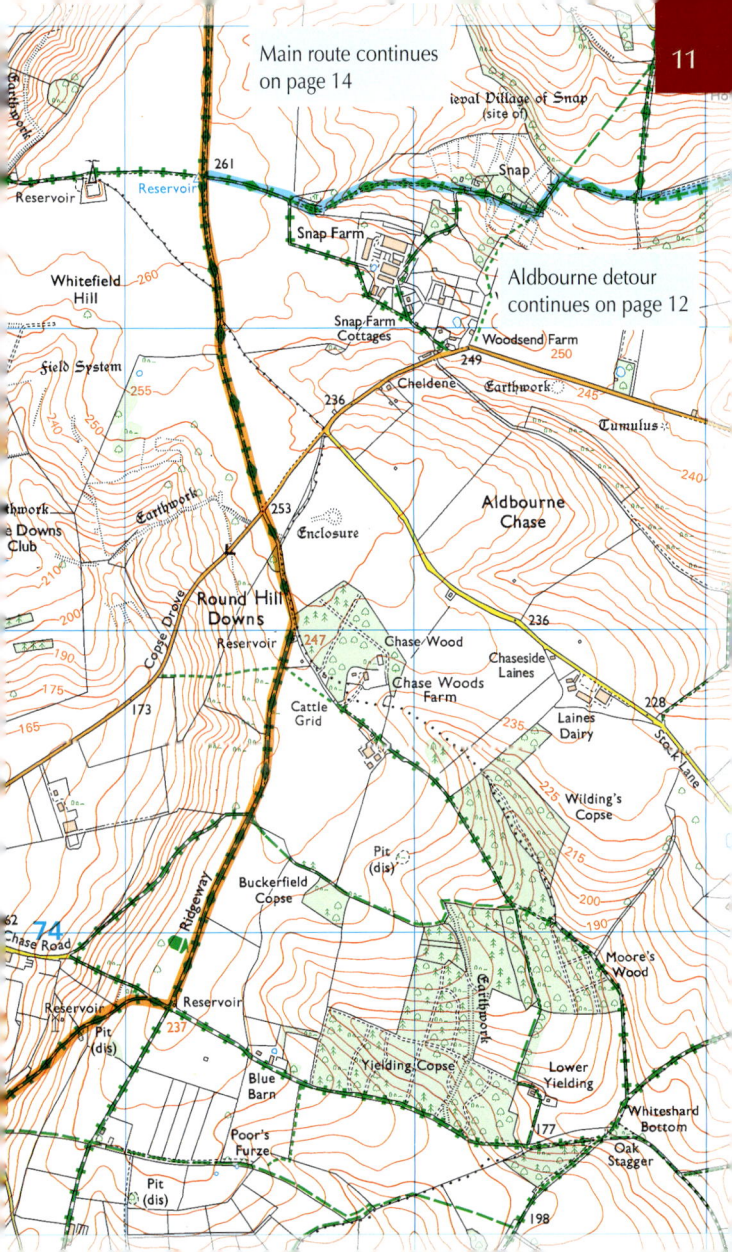

Main route continues
on page 14

ieval Dillage of Snap
(site of)

Snap

Reservoir

Reservoir

Snap Farm

Aldbourne detour
continues on page 12

Whitefield
Hill

260

Snap Farm
Cottages

Woodsend Farm

250

Cheldene

249

236

Earthwork

245

Field System

255

240
250

Tumulus

Earthwork

253

Aldbourne
Chase

240

Downs
Club

270

Enclosure

200

Round Hill
Downs

236

Copse Drove

190

Reservoir

247

Chase Wood

Chaseside
Laines

228

175

Chase Woods
Farm

Laines
Dairy

Stock Lane

165

173

Cattle
Grid

235

225

Wilding's
Copse

Pit
(dis)

215

Ridgeway

Buckerfield
Copse

200

190

Moore's
Wood

62
Chase Road

74

Reservoir

Reservoir

Earthwork

Pit
(dis)

237

Lower
Yielding

Yielding Copse

Whiteshard
Bottom

Blue
Barn

177

Oak
Stagger

Poor's
Furze

Pit
(dis)

198

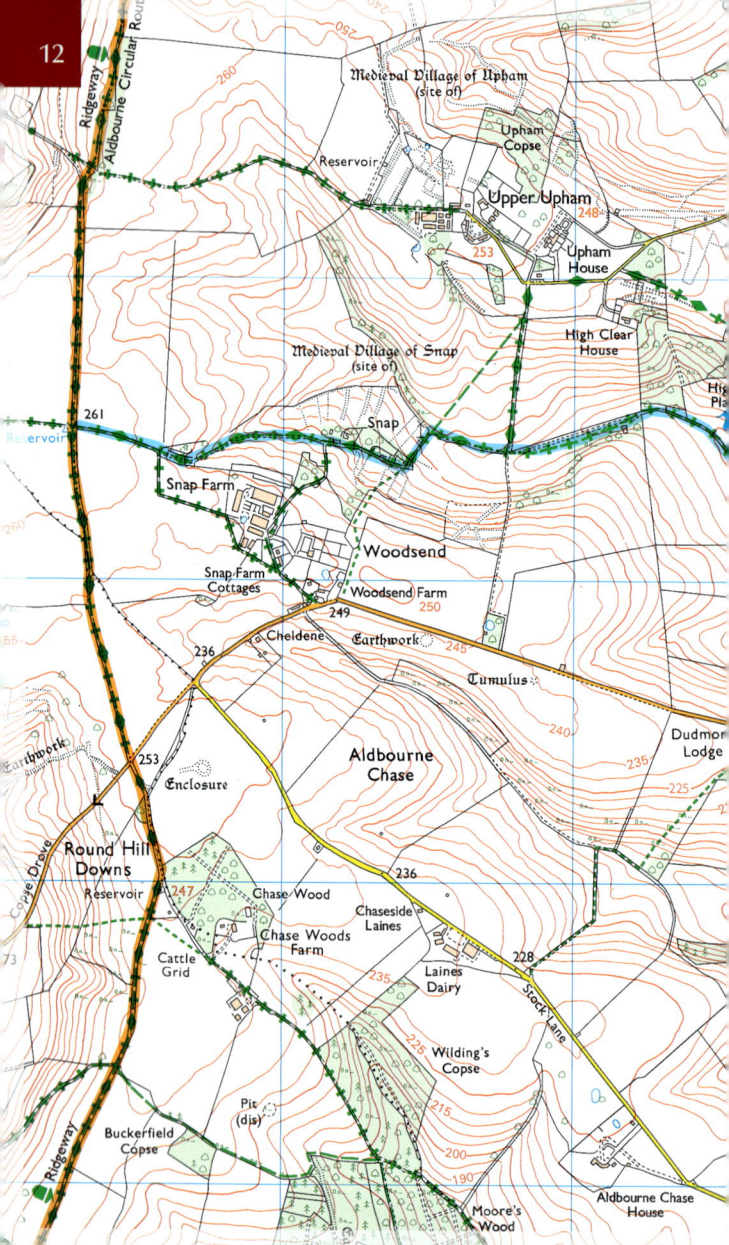

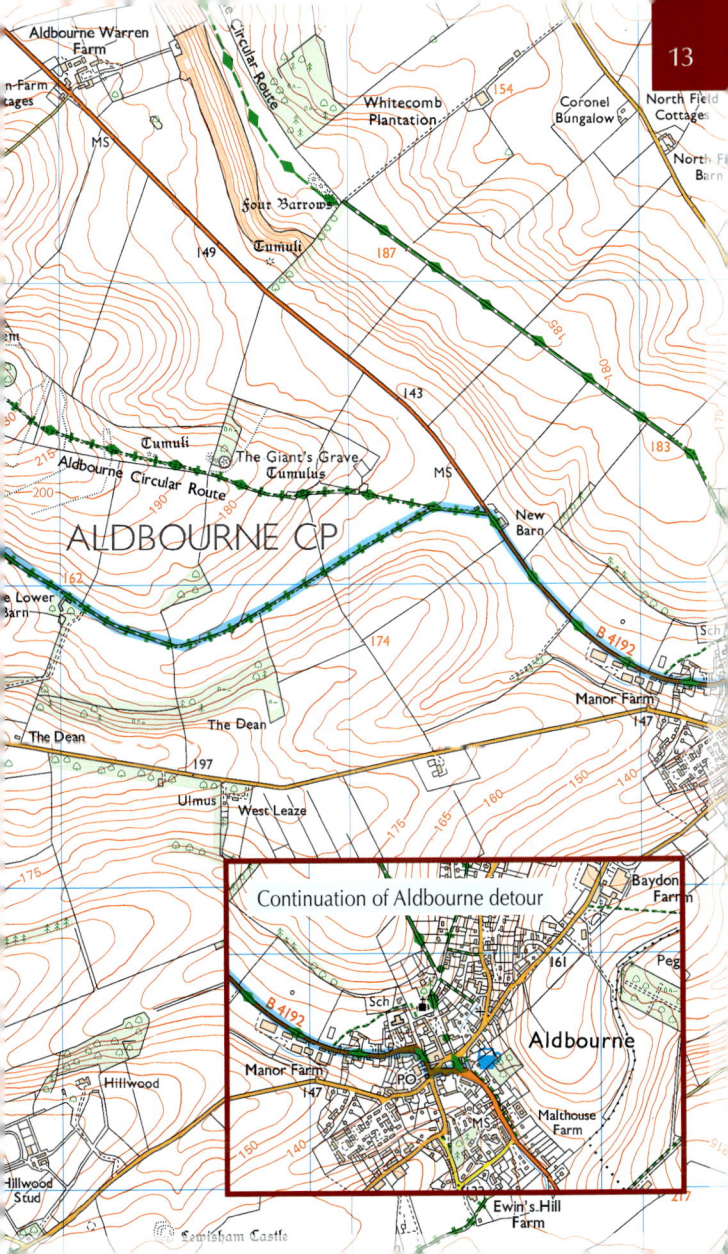

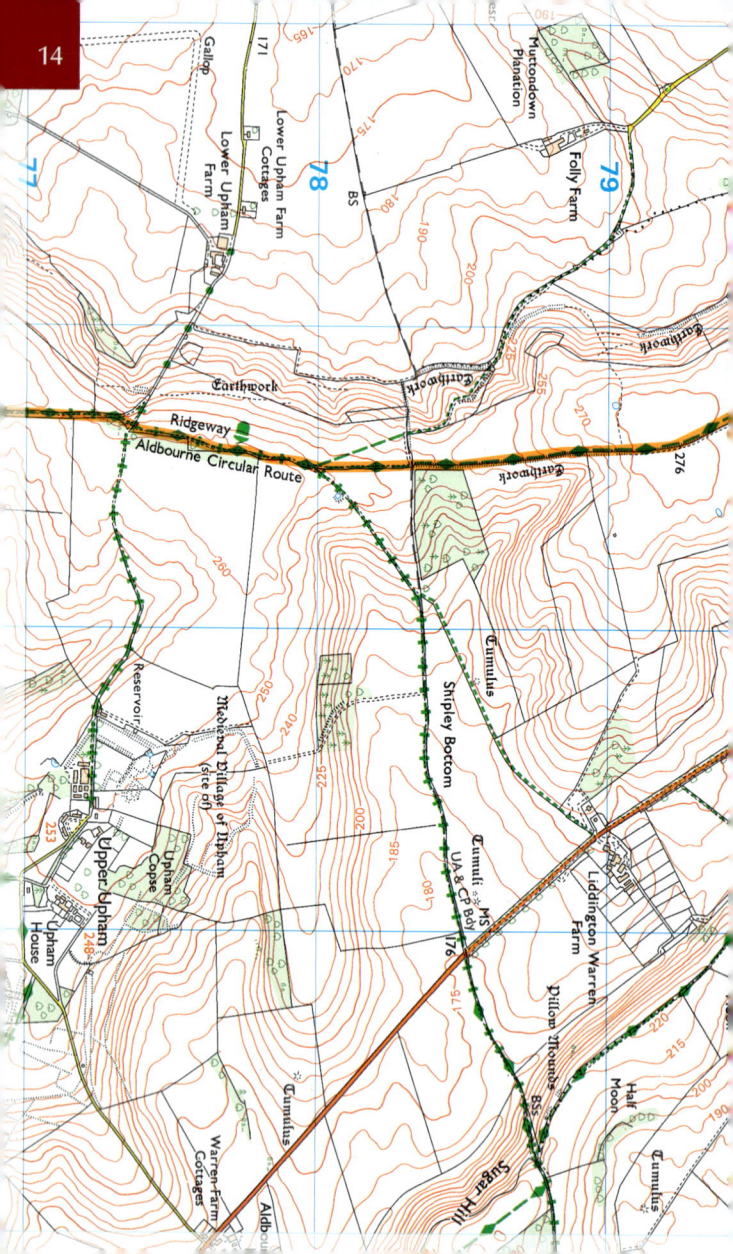

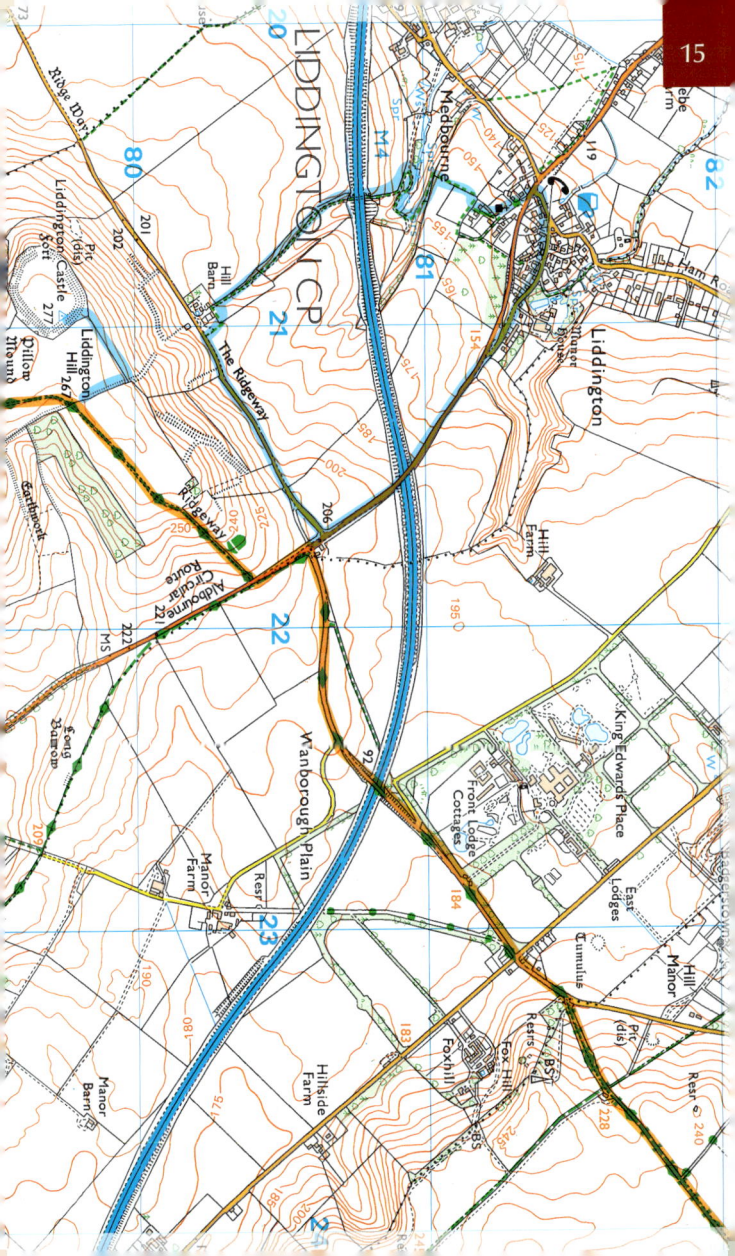

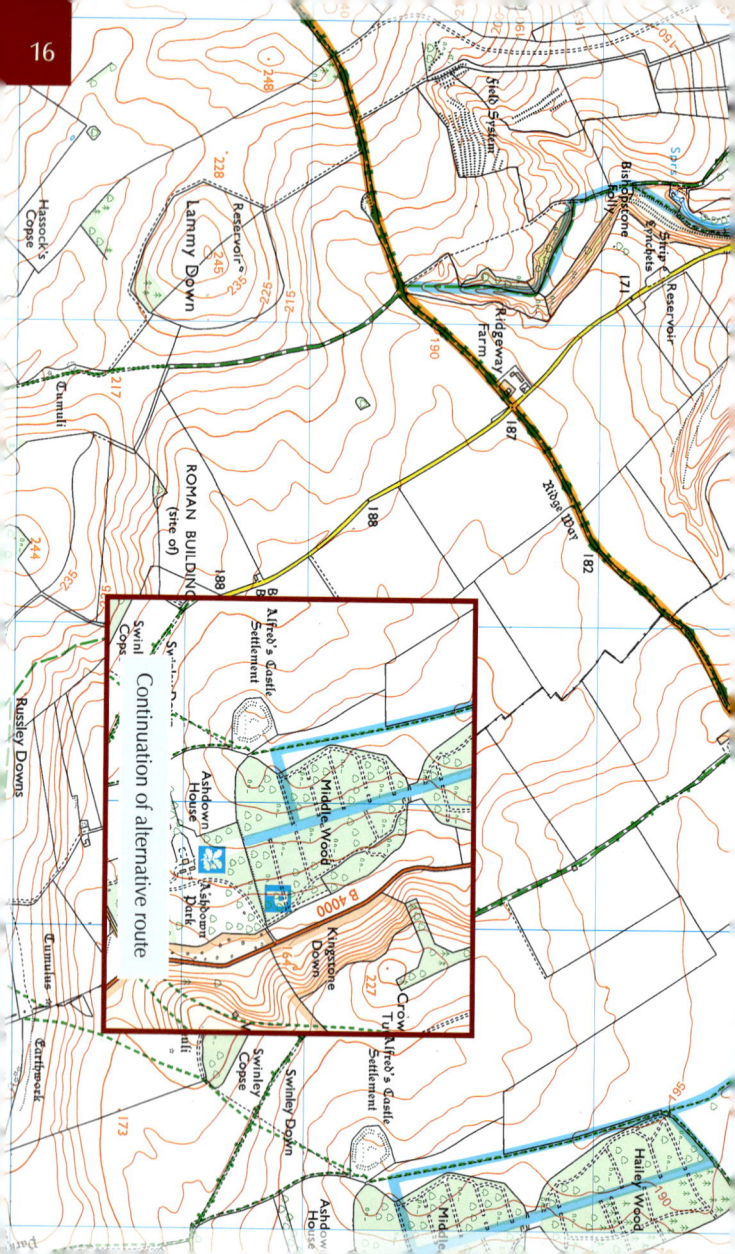

Continuation of alternative route

Ashbury Folly to the A338 Wantage

Start   Ashbury Folly, B4000 (SU 273 843)

Finish   A338, Wantage/Court Hill Centre (SU 394 844)

Distance   13.7km (8.5 miles)

Walking time   4hr 15min

Ashbury Folly to Ogbourne St George

Start   Ashbury Folly, B4000 (SU 273 843)

Finish   Near Ogbourne St George (SU 192 746)

Distance   17.3km (10.7 miles)

Walking time   5hr 30min

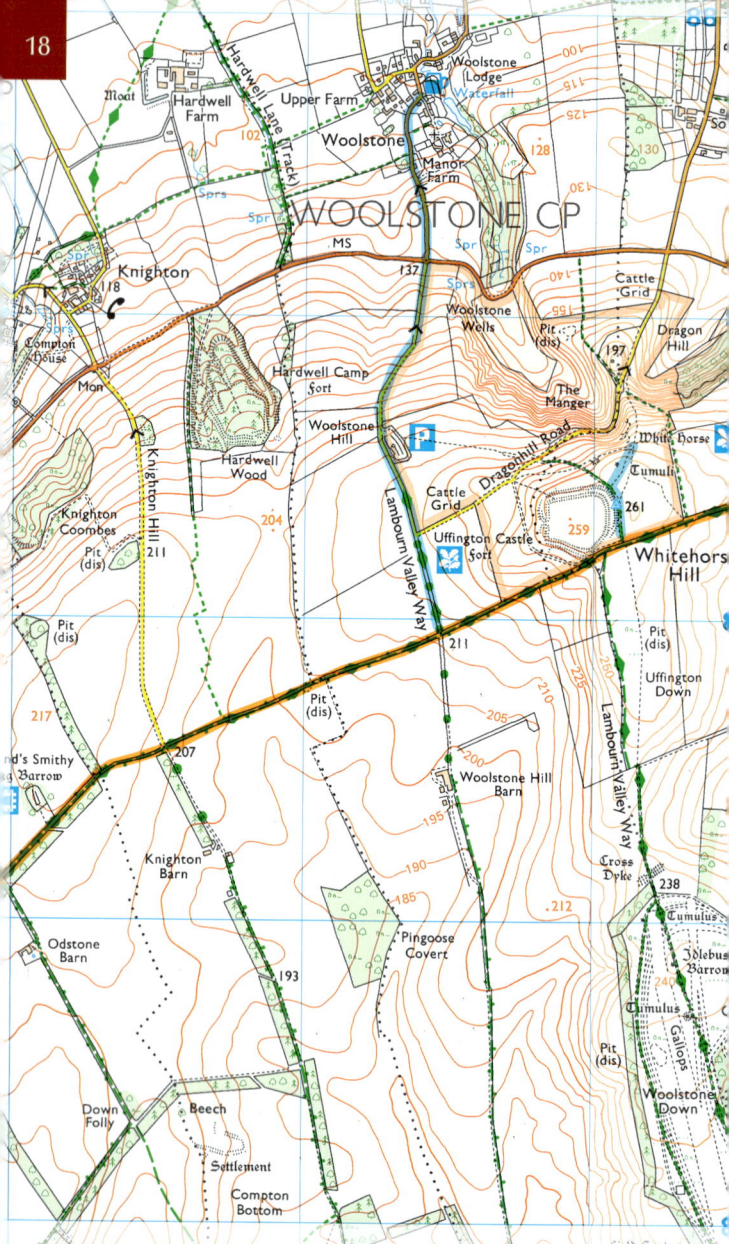

Moat
Hardwell
Farm
Upper Farm
Woolstone
Lodge
Woolstone
Waterfall
Hardwell Lane (Track)
102
Manor
Farm
WOOLSTONE CP
Spr
Spr
MS
137
Spr
Spr
Knighton
18
Compton
House
Mon
Woolstone
Wells
Pit
(dis)
197
Cattle
Grid
Dragon
Hill
Hardwell Camp
Fort
Woolstone
Hill
The
Manger
White Horse
P
Lambourn Valley Way
Hardwell
Wood
Cattle
Grid
Dragonhill Road
Tumuli
Knighton
Coombes
204
Uffington Castle
Fort
259
261
Whitehors
Hill
Knighton Hill
Pit
(dis)
211
Pit
(dis)
211
Pit
(dis)
Uffington
Down
217
Pit
(dis)
205
210
Lambourn Valley Way
d's Smithy
Barrow
207
200
195
Knighton
Barn
Woolstone Hill
Barn
Cross
Dyke
238
Odstone
Barn
190
212
Tumulus
193
185
Pingoose
Covert
Idlebus
Barrow
Tumulus
Pit
(dis)
Woolstone
Down
Down
Folly
Beech
Gallops
Settlement
Compton
Bottom

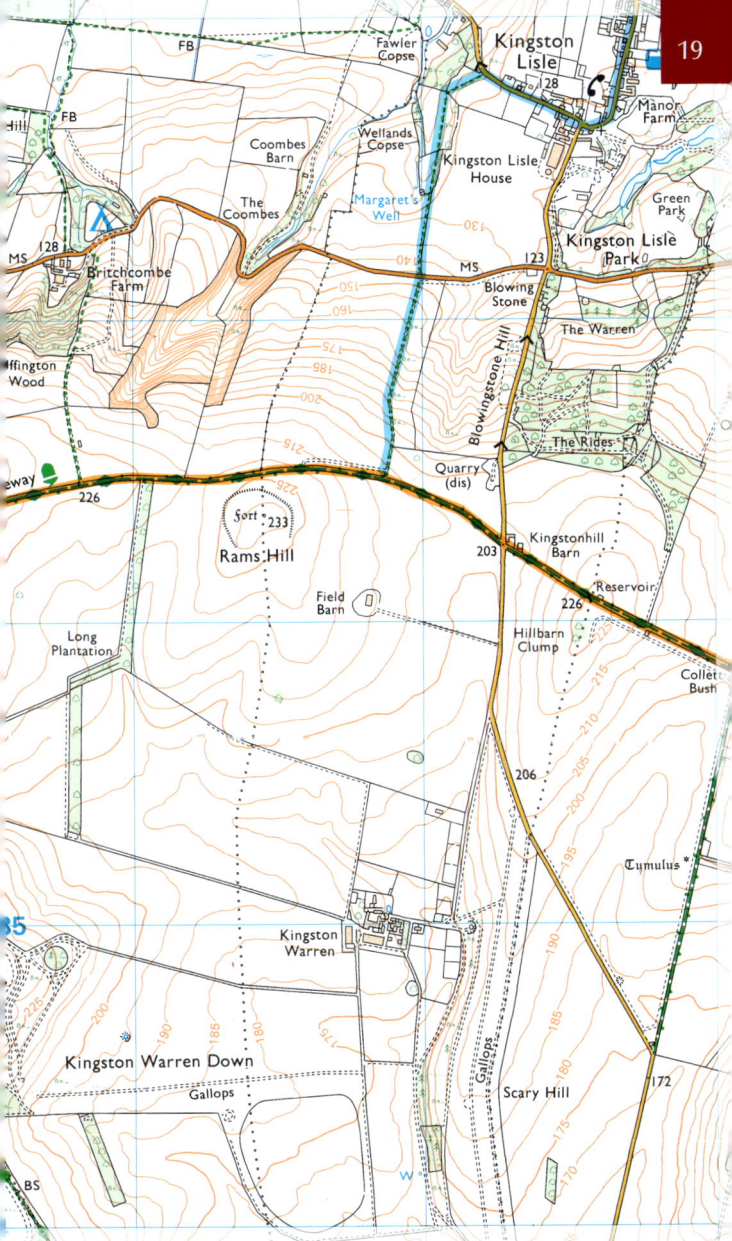

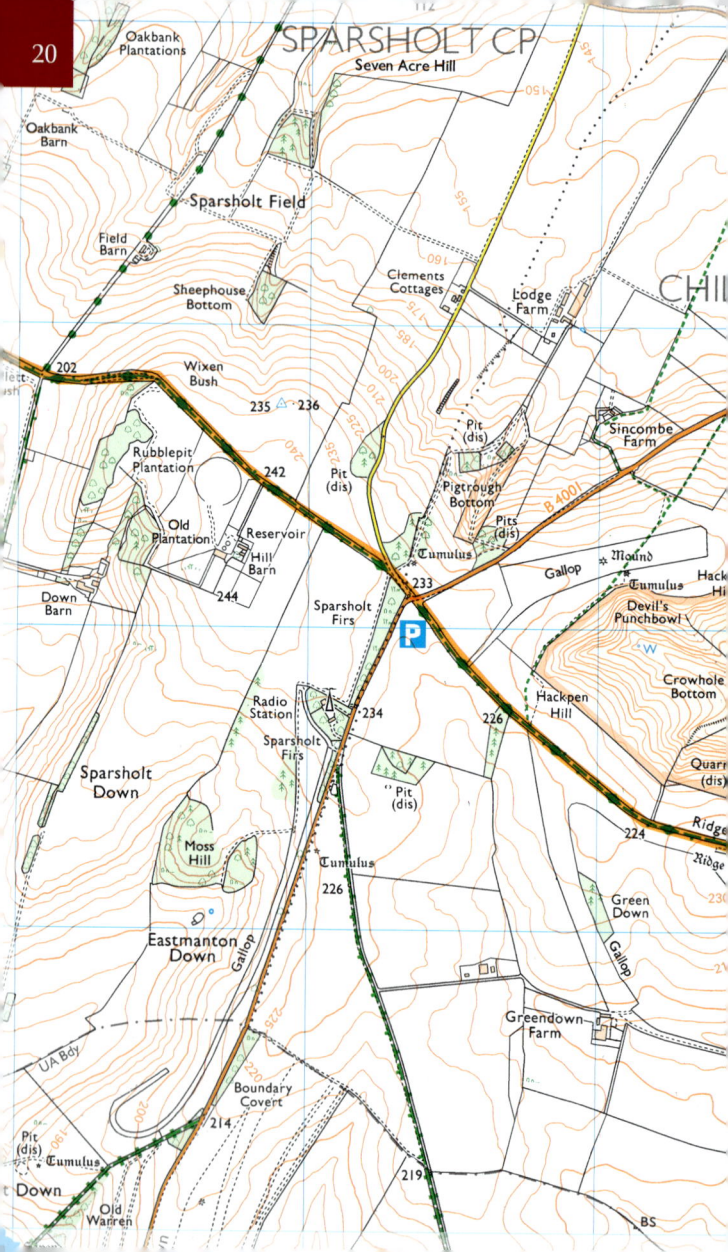

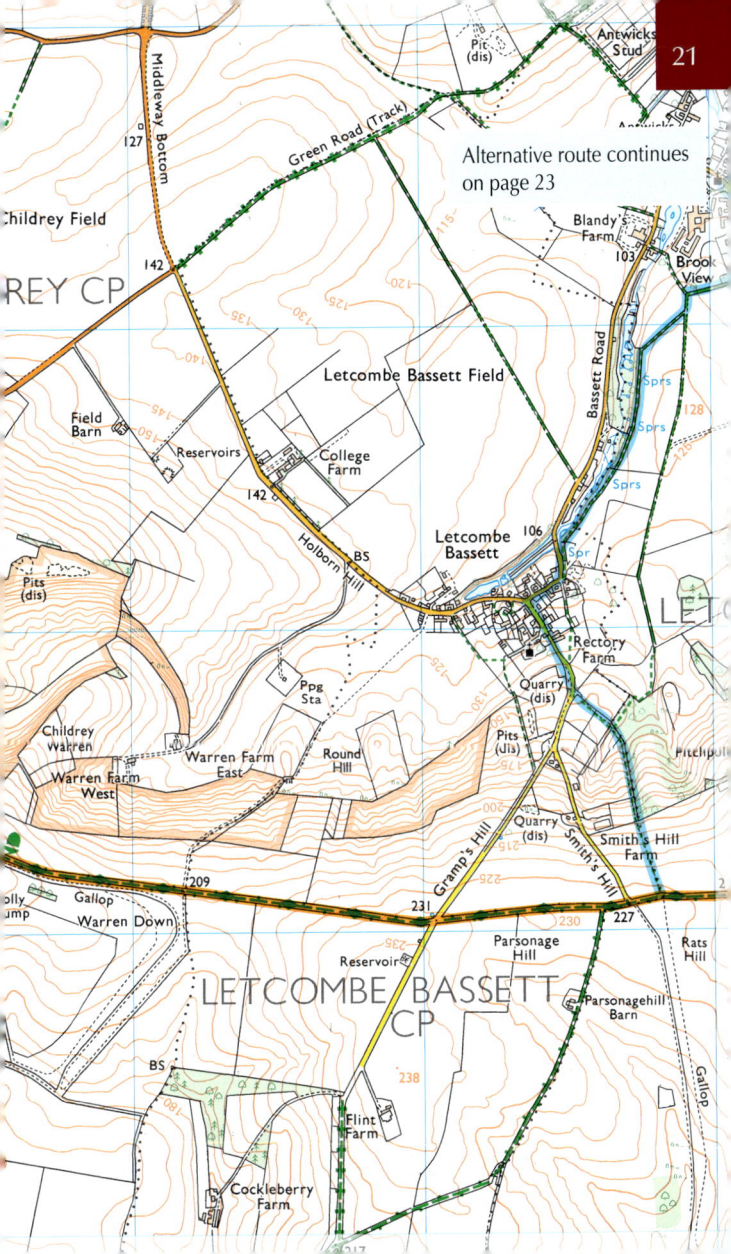

Alternative route continues
on page 23

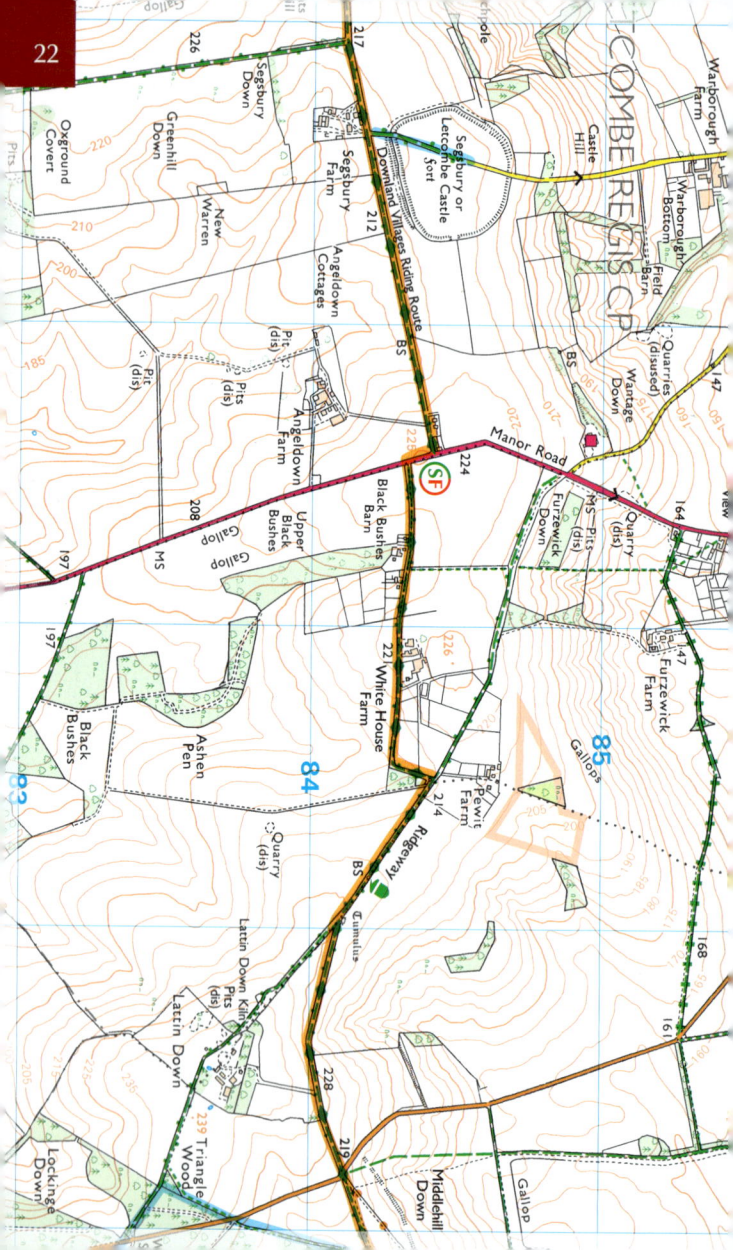

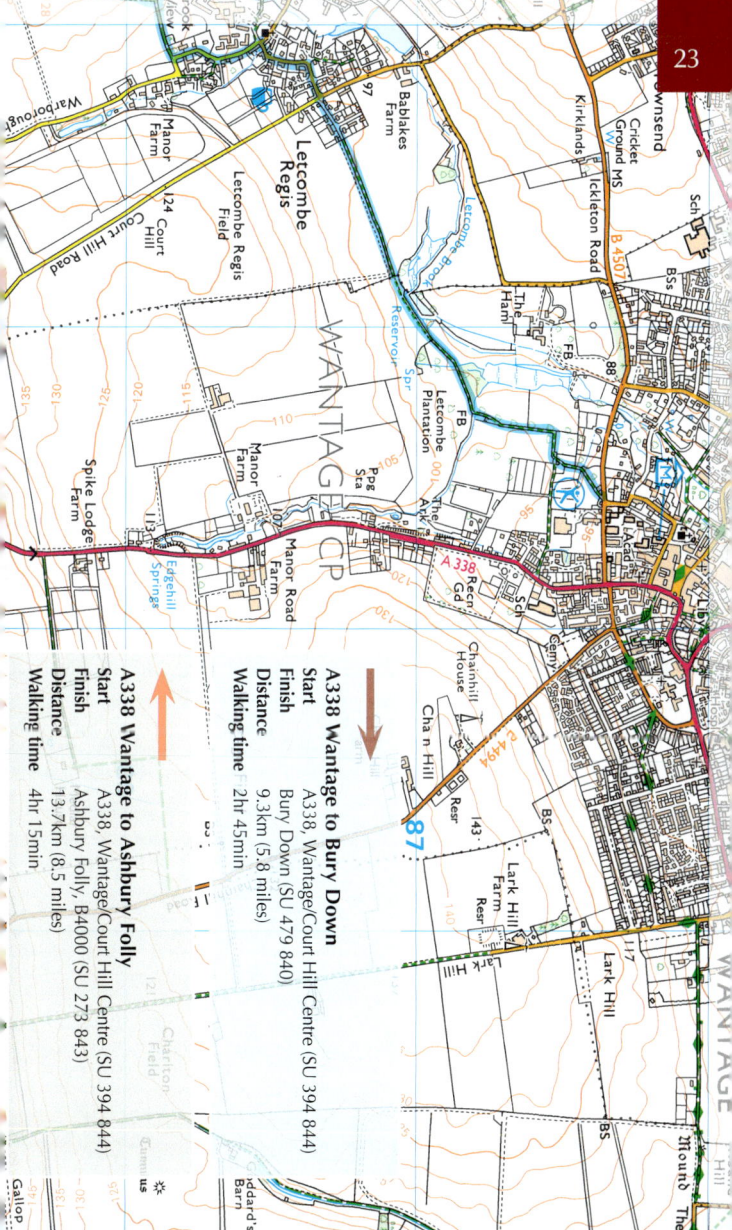

A338 Wantage to Bury Down

Start A338, Wantage/Court Hill Centre (SU 394 844)
Finish Bury Down (SU 479 840)
Distance 9.3km (5.8 miles)
Walking time 2hr 45min

A338 Wantage to Ashbury Folly

Start A338, Wantage/Court Hill Centre (SU 394 844)
Finish Ashbury Folly, B4000 (SU 273 843)
Distance 13.7km (8.5 miles)
Walking time 4hr 15min

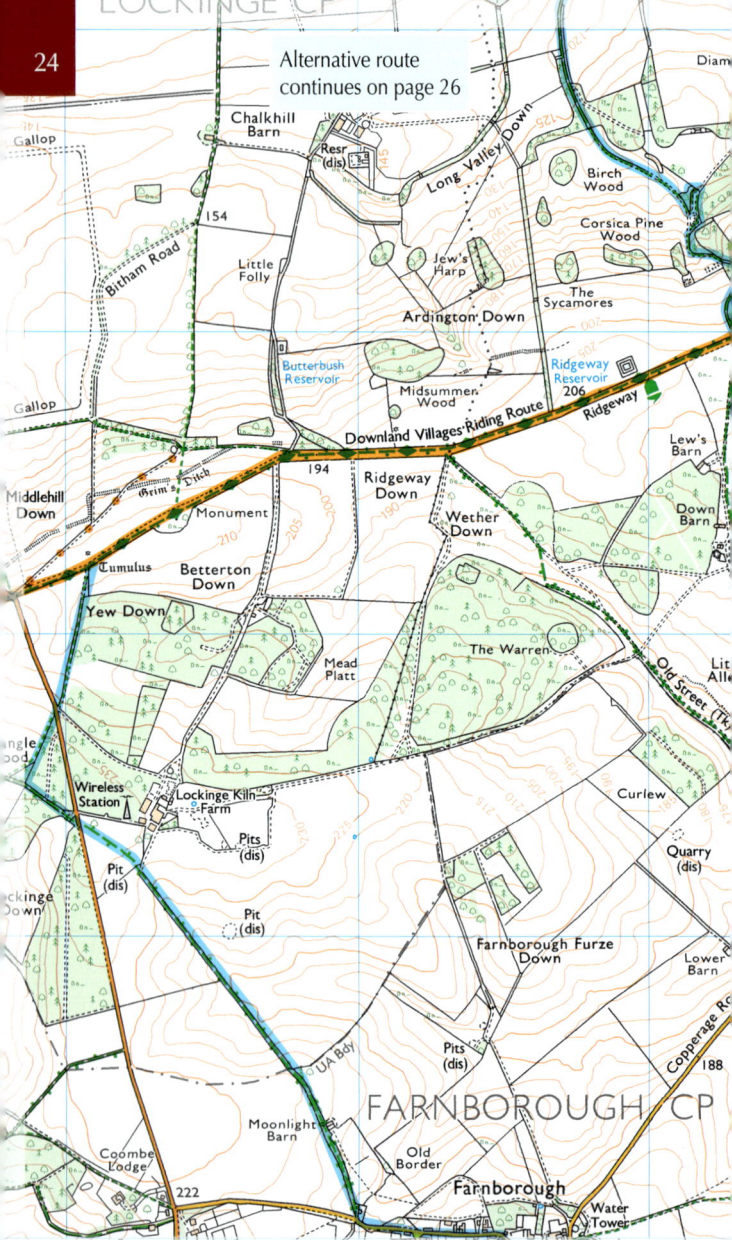

Alternative route
continues on page 26

LOCKINGE CP

Gallop

Chalkhill
Barn

Resr
(dis)

Long Valley Down

Birch
Wood

Diam

Corsica Pine
Wood

154

Bitham Road

Little
Folly

Jew's
Harp

The
Sycamores

Ardington Down

Butterbush
Reservoir

Ridgeway
Reservoir
206

Gallop

Midsummer
Wood

Downland Villages Riding Route

Ridgeway

Middlehill
Down

Grim's Ditch

194

Monument

Ridgeway
Down

Wether
Down

Lew's
Barn

Down
Barn

Tumulus

Betterton
Down

Yew Down

Mead
Platt

The Warren

Old Street (Tk)

Lit
All

ngle
ood

Wireless
Station

Lockinge Kiln
Farm

Pits
(dis)

Curlew

Quarry
(dis)

Pit
(dis)

Pit
(dis)

Farnborough Furze
Down

Lower
Barn

kinge
own

UA Bdy

Pits
(dis)

FARNBOROUGH CP

188

Copperage Rd

Coombe
Lodge

222

Moonlight
Barn

Old
Border

Farnborough

Water
Tower

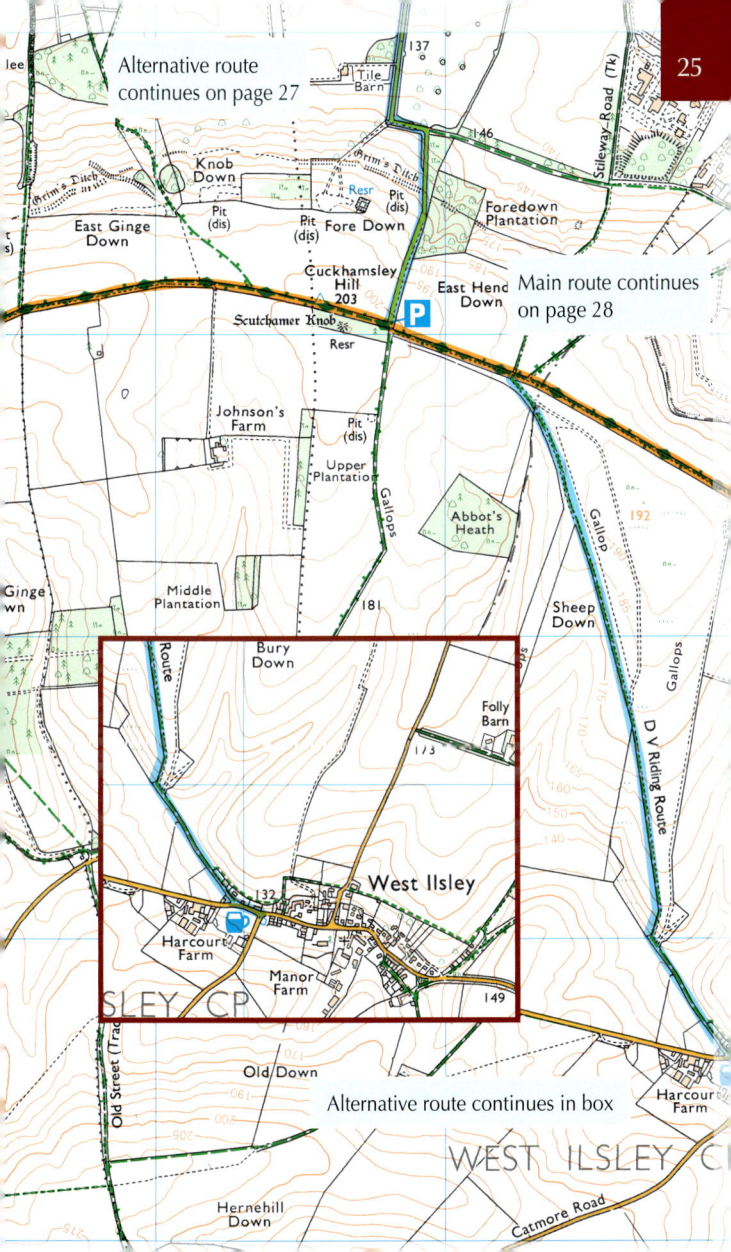

Alternative route continues on page 27

Main route continues on page 28

Alternative route continues in box

Tile Barn

137

146

Knob Down

Grim's Ditch

Resr

Pit (dis)

Pit (dis)

Fore Down

Foredown Plantation

East Ginge Down

Grim's Ditch

Pit (dis)

Pit (dis)

Cuckhamsley Hill 203

Scutchamer Knob

Resr

East Hendred Down

P

Johnson's Farm

Pit (dis)

Upper Plantation

Gallops

Abbot's Heath

192

Gallop

Ginge wn

Middle Plantation

181

Sheep Down

Gallop

Gallops

D V Riding Route

Route

Bury Down

Folly Barn

173

165

150

140

West Ilsley

132

Harcourt Farm

Manor Farm

149

SLEY CP

Old Street (Trac

Old Down

170

190

205

WEST ILSLEY C

Harcourt Farm

Hernehill Down

Catmore Road

Stileway Road (Tk)

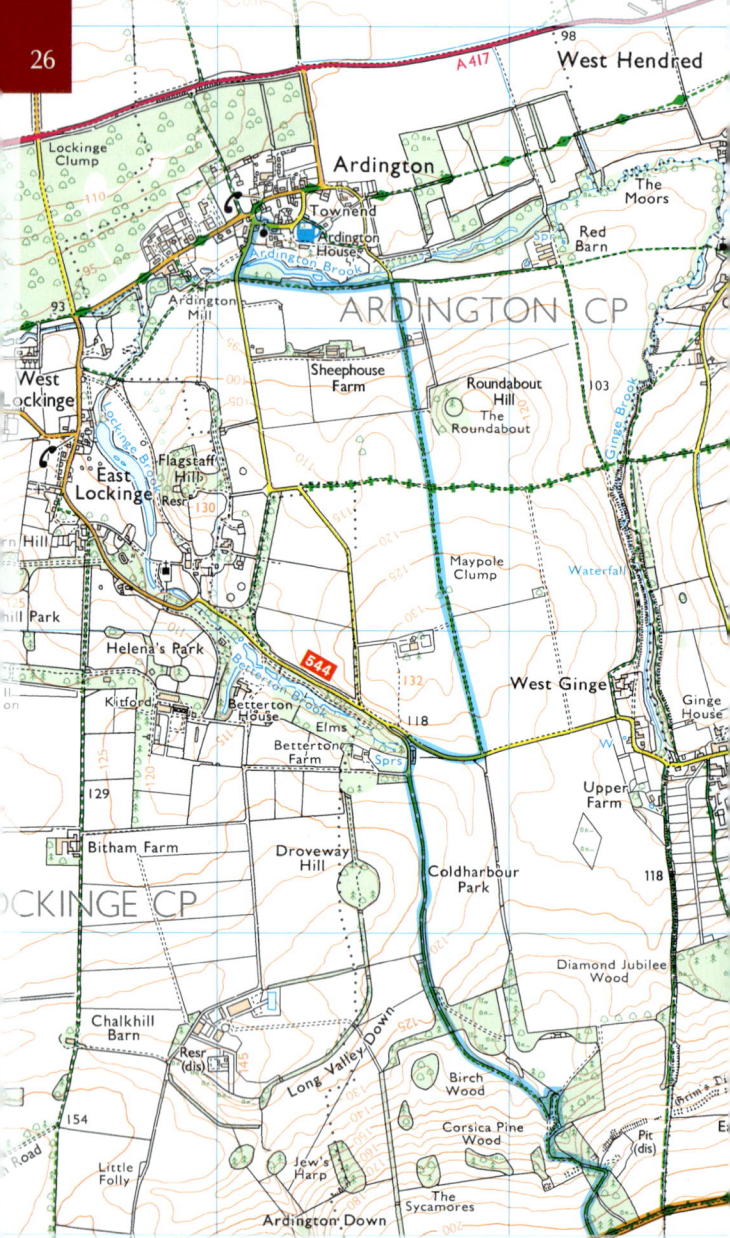

West Hendred

A 417

98

Lockinge
Clump

Ardington

Townend

Ardington
House

Ardington Brook

110

95

93

West
Lockinge

Ardington
Mill

The
Moors

Red
Barn

Spr

ARDINGTON CP

Sheephouse
Farm

Roundabout
Hill
The
Roundabout

103

Ginge Brook

East
Lockinge

Flagstaff
Hill
Resr

130

n Hill

Maypole
Clump

Waterfall

ill Park

Helena's Park

Kitford

Betterton
House

Betterton
Brook

544

Elms

Betterton
Farm

Sprs

118

West Ginge

Ginge
House

021

132

125

120

129

Upper
Farm

118

Bitham Farm

Droveway
Hill

Coldharbour
Park

LOCKINGE CP

Diamond Jubilee
Wood

Chalkhill
Barn

Resr
(dis)

Long Valley Down

125

Birch
Wood

Pit
(dis)

E

154

Little
Folly

Jew's
Harp

Corsica Pine
Wood

The
Sycamores

Ardington Down

n Road

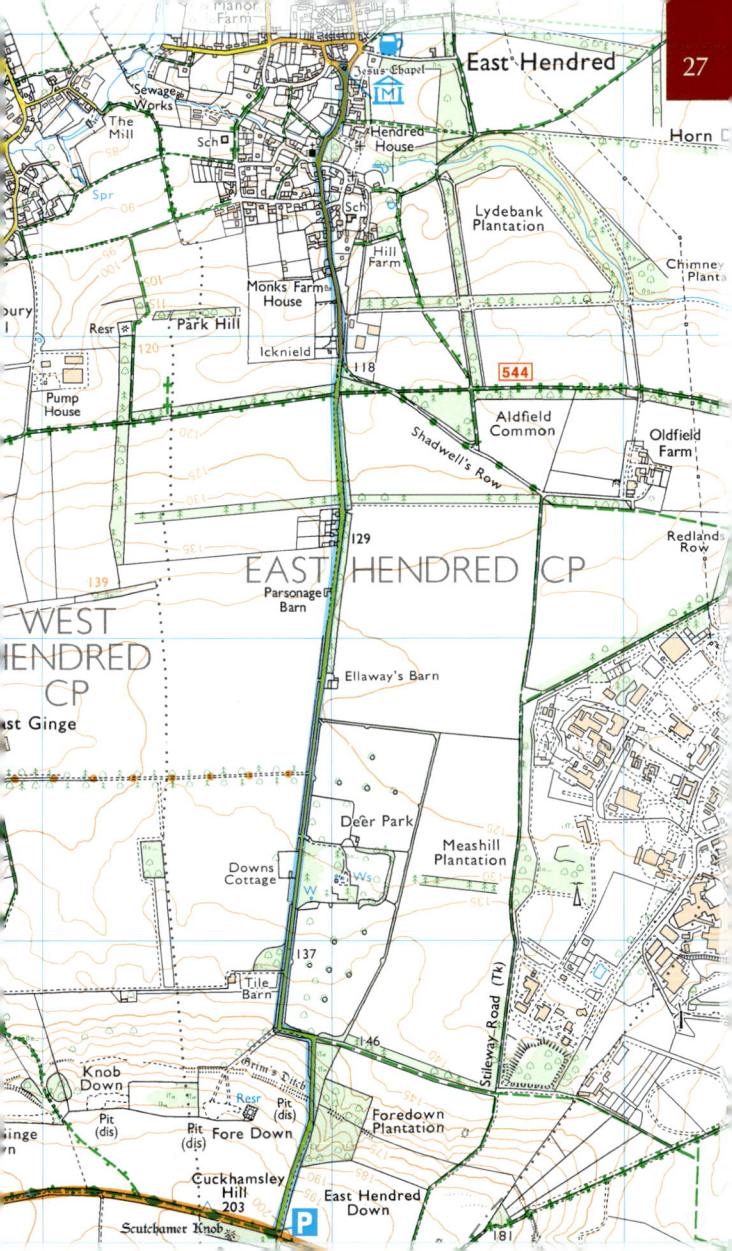

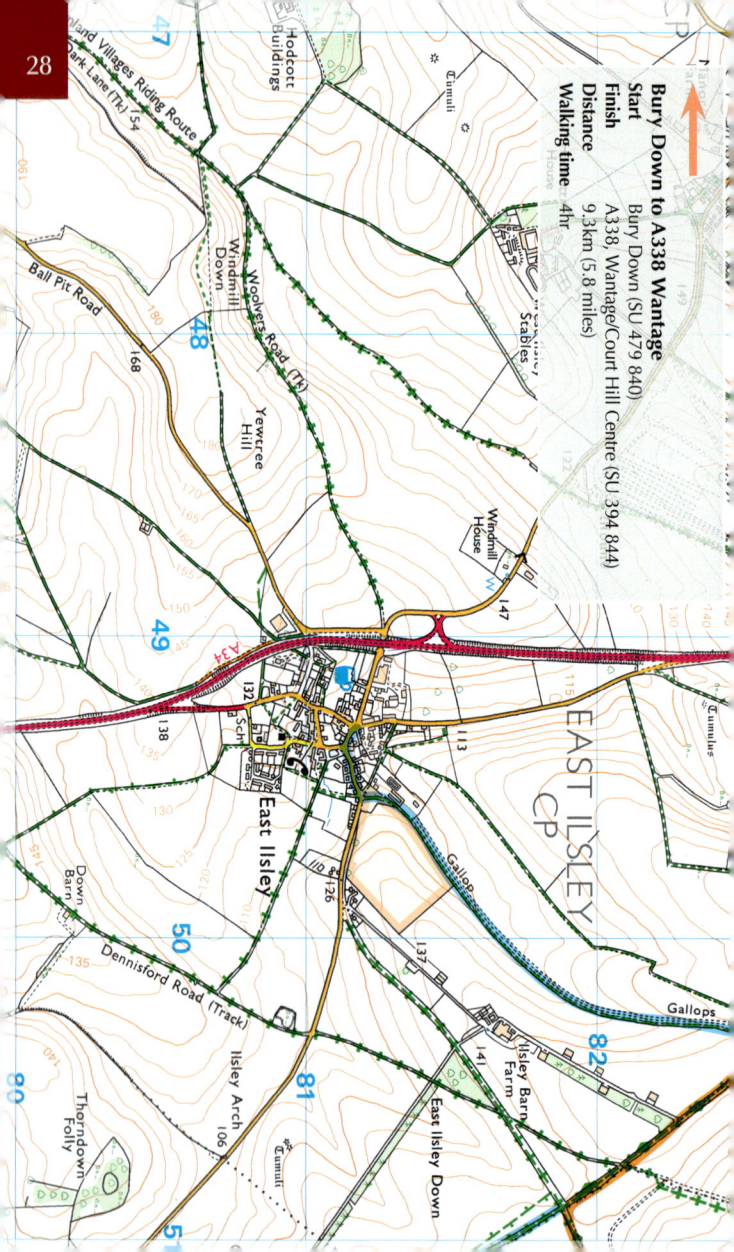

Bury Down to A338 Wantage

Start   Bury Down (SU 479 840)
Finish   A338, Wantage/Court Hill Centre (SU 394 844)
Distance   9.3km (5.8 miles)
Walking time 4hr

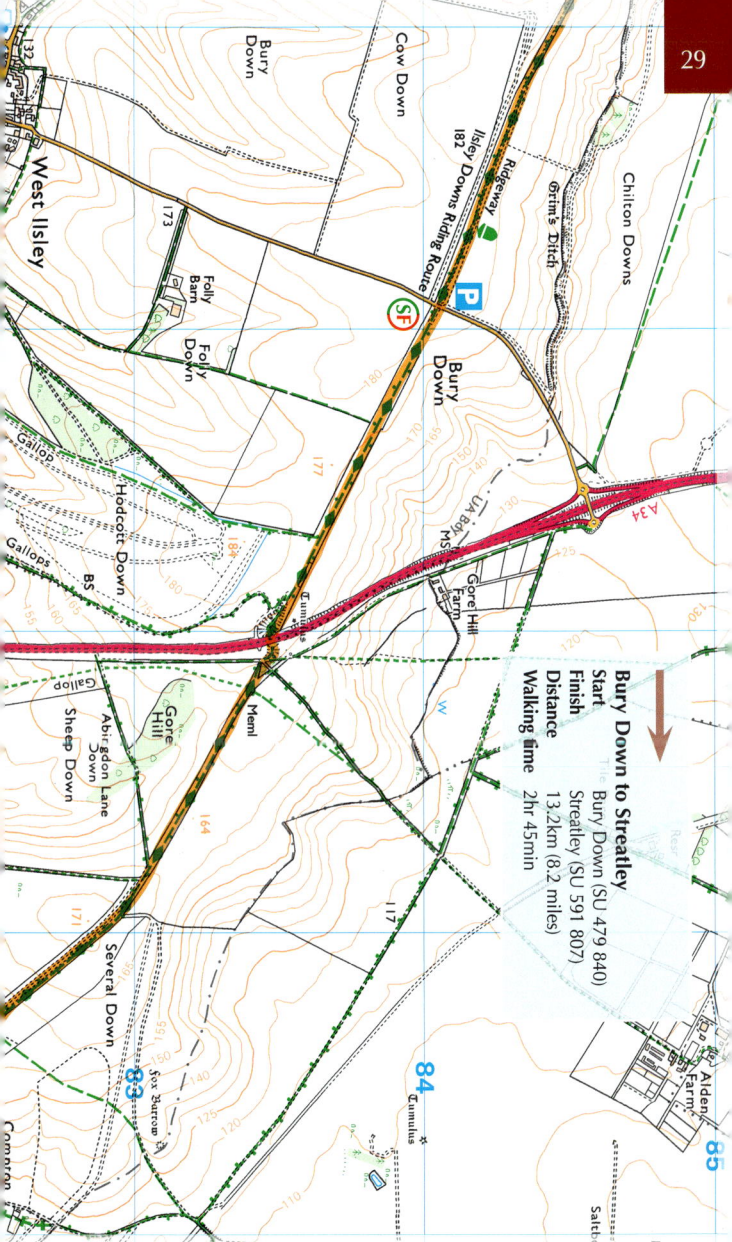

Bury Down to Streatley

Start Bury Down (SU 479 840)
Finish Streatley (SU 591 807)
Distance 13.2km (8.2 miles)
Walking Time 2hr 45min

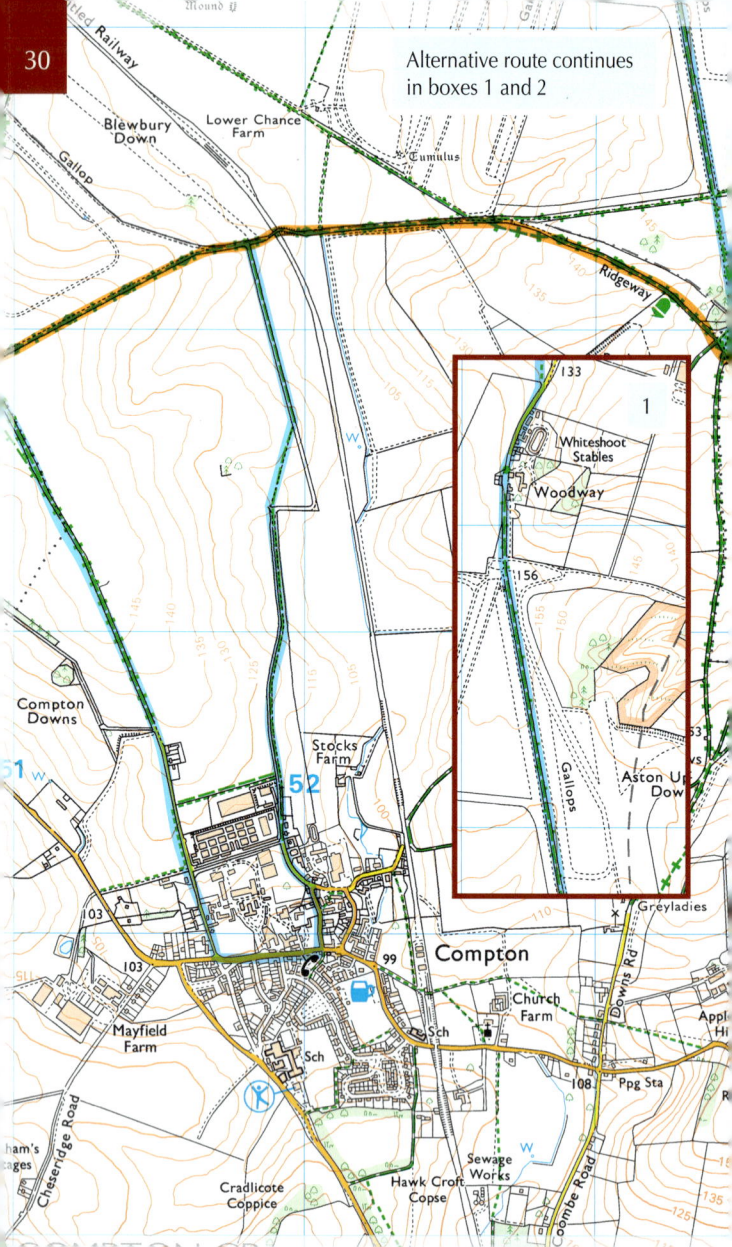

Alternative route continues
in boxes 1 and 2

Blewbury
Down

Lower Chance
Farm

Gallop

Tumulus

Ridgeway

133

1

Whiteshoot
Stables

Woodway

156

156

Compton
Downs

Stocks
Farm

51 W

52

Gallops

Aston U
Dow

Greyladies

03

Mayfield
Farm

103

99

Compton

Church
Farm

Sch

Sch

108

Ppg Sta

Appl
Hi

Downs Rd

Coombe Road

Chesleridge Road

Cradlicote
Coppice

Hawk Croft
Copse

Sewage
Works

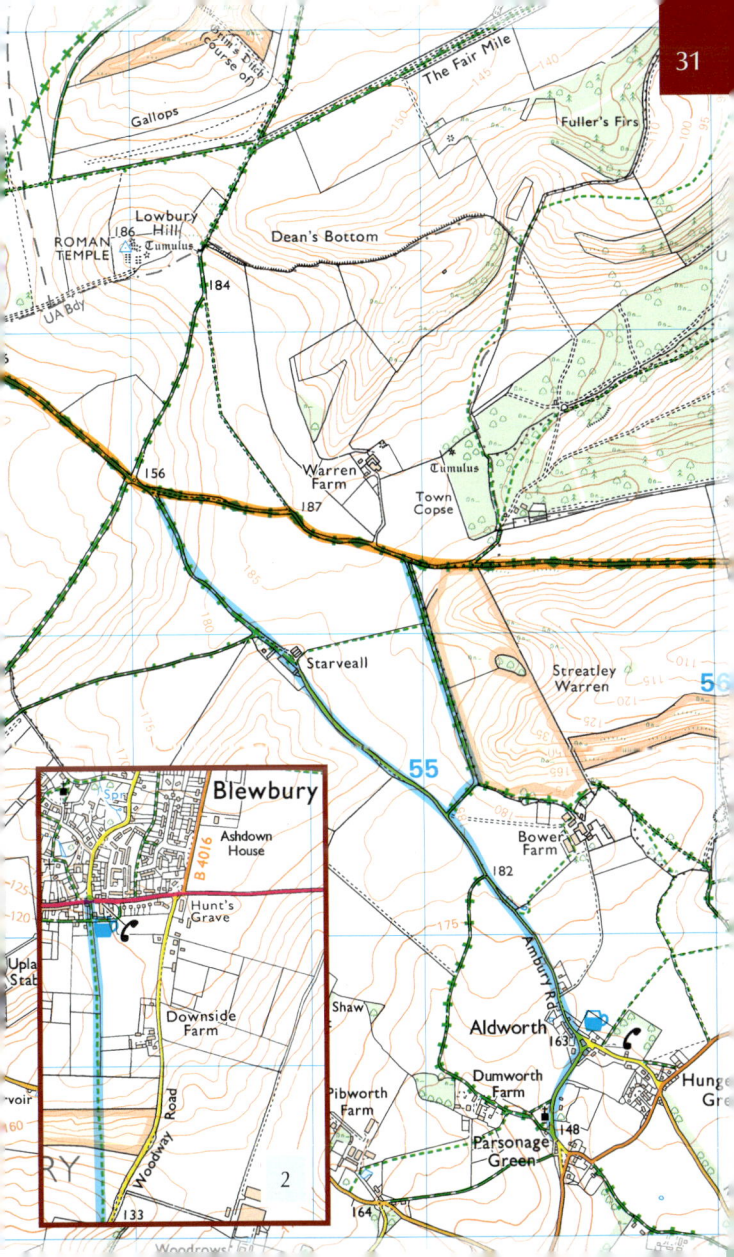

The Fair Mile

Gallops

Fuller's Firs

Lowbury
Hill

ROMAN
TEMPLE

186 Tumulus

Dean's Bottom

184

UA Bdy

156

Warren
Farm

187

Tumulus

Town
Copse

Starveall

Streatley
Warren

55

56

Bower
Farm

182

Blewbury

Ashdown
House

B 4016

Hunt's
Grave

Upla
Stab

Aldworth

163

Downside
Farm

Shaw

Dumworth
Farm

Woodway Road

Pibworth
Farm

148

Ambury Rd

Hunge
Gre

voir

160

RY

Parsonage
Green

2

133

164

Woodrow

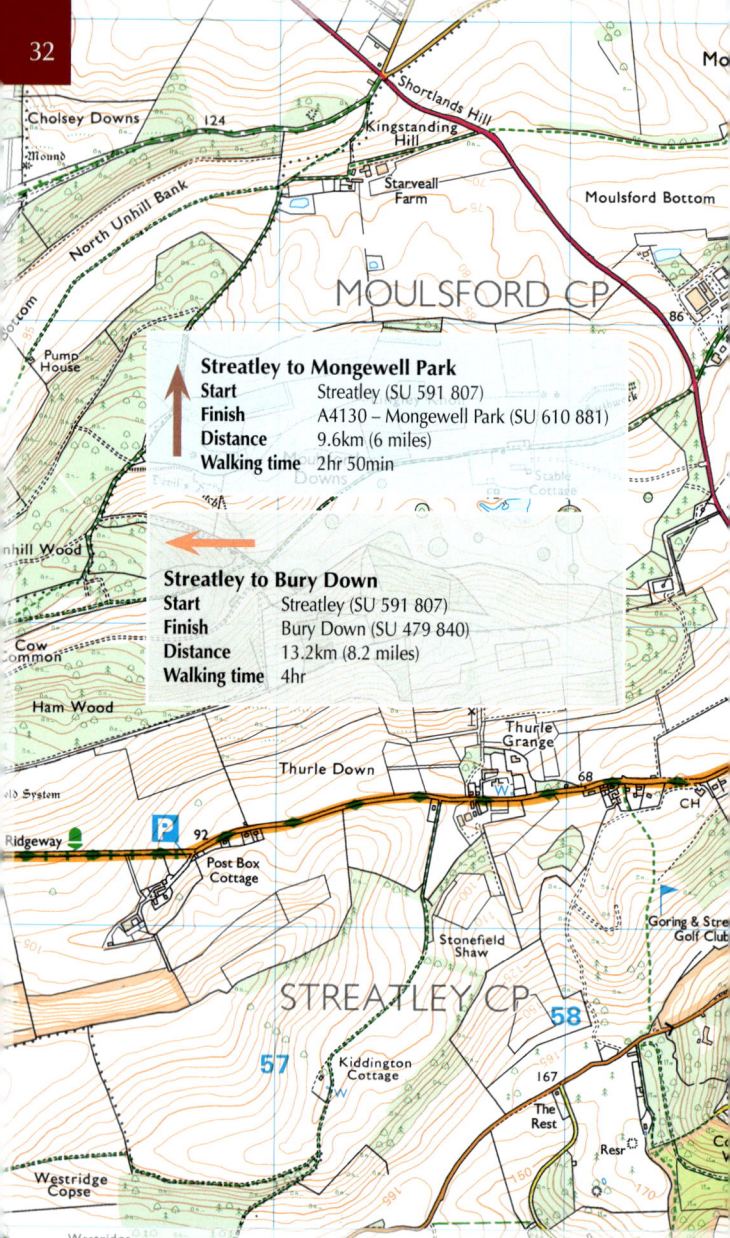

Streatley to Mongewell Park

Start	Streatley (SU 591 807)
Finish	A4130 – Mongewell Park (SU 610 881)
Distance	9.6km (6 miles)
Walking time	2hr 50min

Streatley to Bury Down

Start	Streatley (SU 591 807)
Finish	Bury Down (SU 479 840)
Distance	13.2km (8.2 miles)
Walking time	4hr

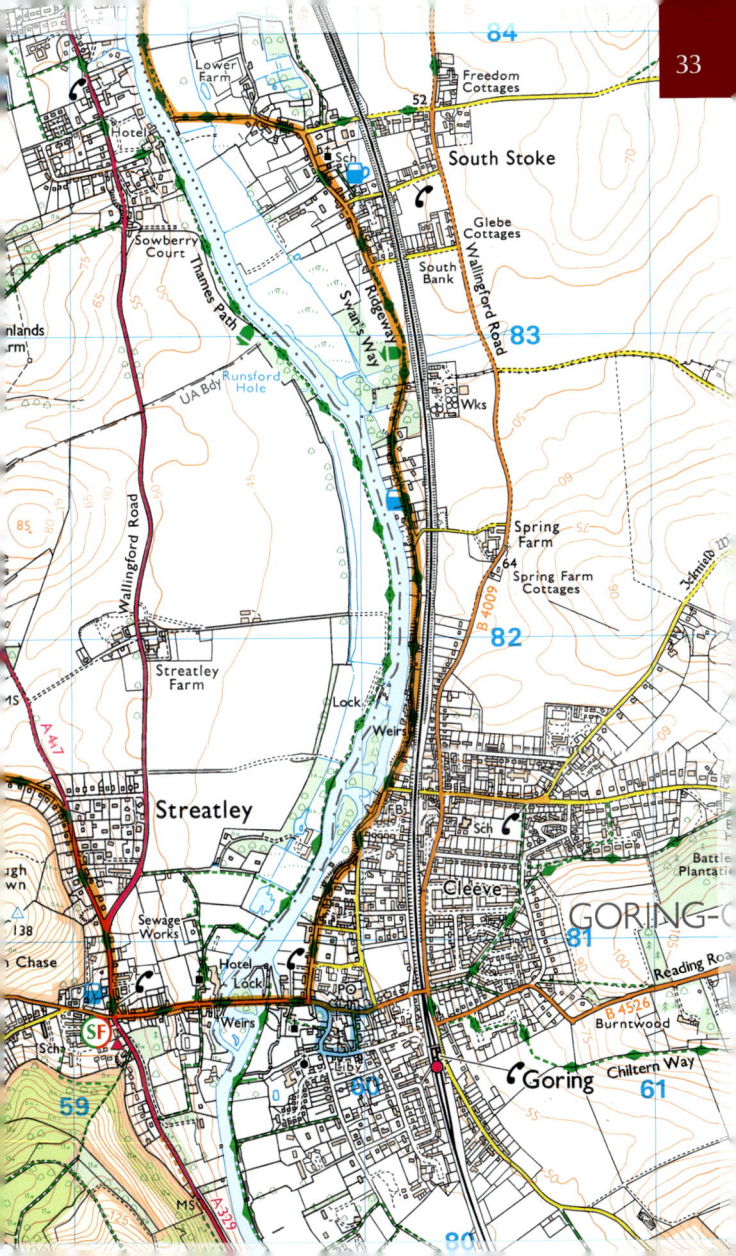

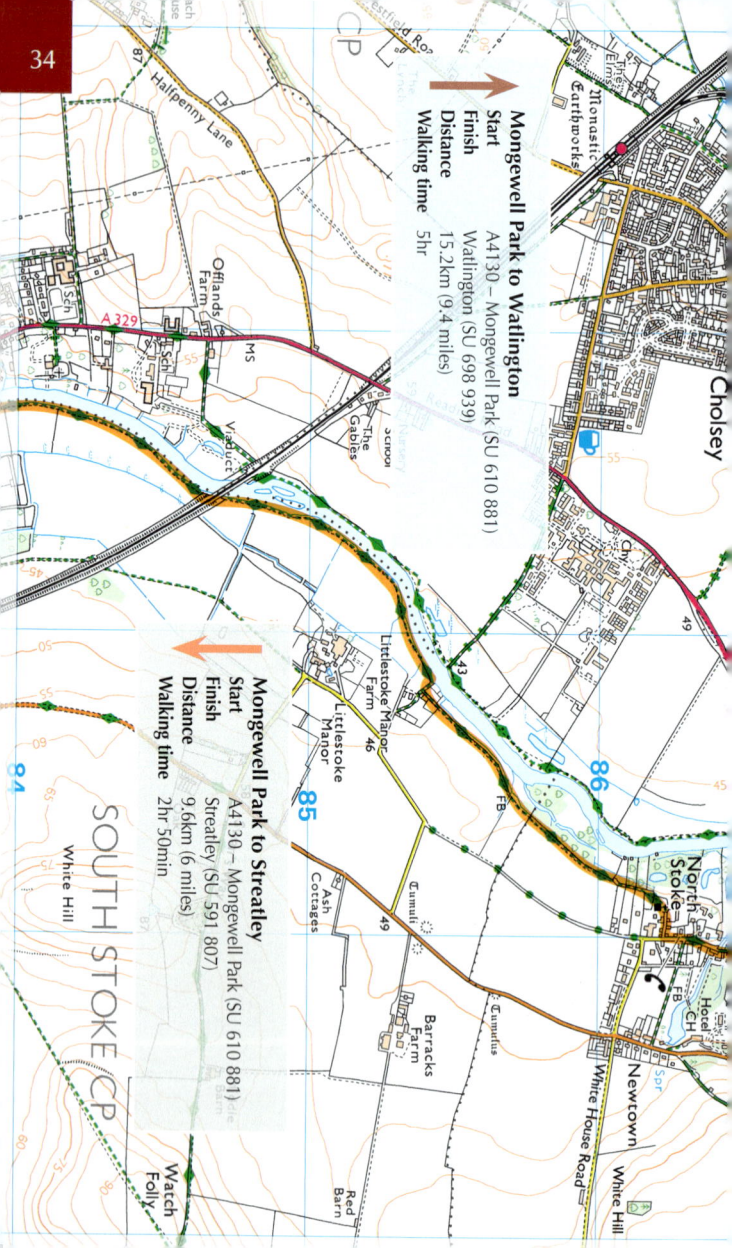

Mongewell Park to Watlington

Start	A4130 – Mongewell Park (SU 610 881)
Finish	Watlington (SU 698 939)
Distance	15.2km (9.4 miles)
Walking time	5hr

Mongewell Park to Streatley

Start	A4130 – Mongewell Park (SU 610 881)
Finish	Streatley (SU 591 807)
Distance	9.6km (6 miles)
Walking time	2hr 50min

Continuation of alternative route

WALLINGFORD

Hithercroft Farm

Inst of
Hydrology

Offices

Newnham
Murren

New Barn
Farm

Wallingford Railway

Cox's
Farm

Blackall's
Farm

The Lodge

Bucklands

Winterbrook

Winterbrook

Bradford's Brook

Bow Barn

Choiseul
Stables

Mead
Furlong

Mill
Court

Reading Road   A329

Bow
Bridge
49

87

Thames Path

White Cross

88

Hosp

River Thames

Carmel
College

Mon

SF

Newnham
Farm

48

The Springs Hotel
and Golf Club

Mongewell
Park

The Lake 66

Mongewell

A4130

Newnham Manor
Farm

Newnham
Murren

Wallingford Road
56

B 4009

Tickledown

Ridgeway

Lark
Rise

90

75

45

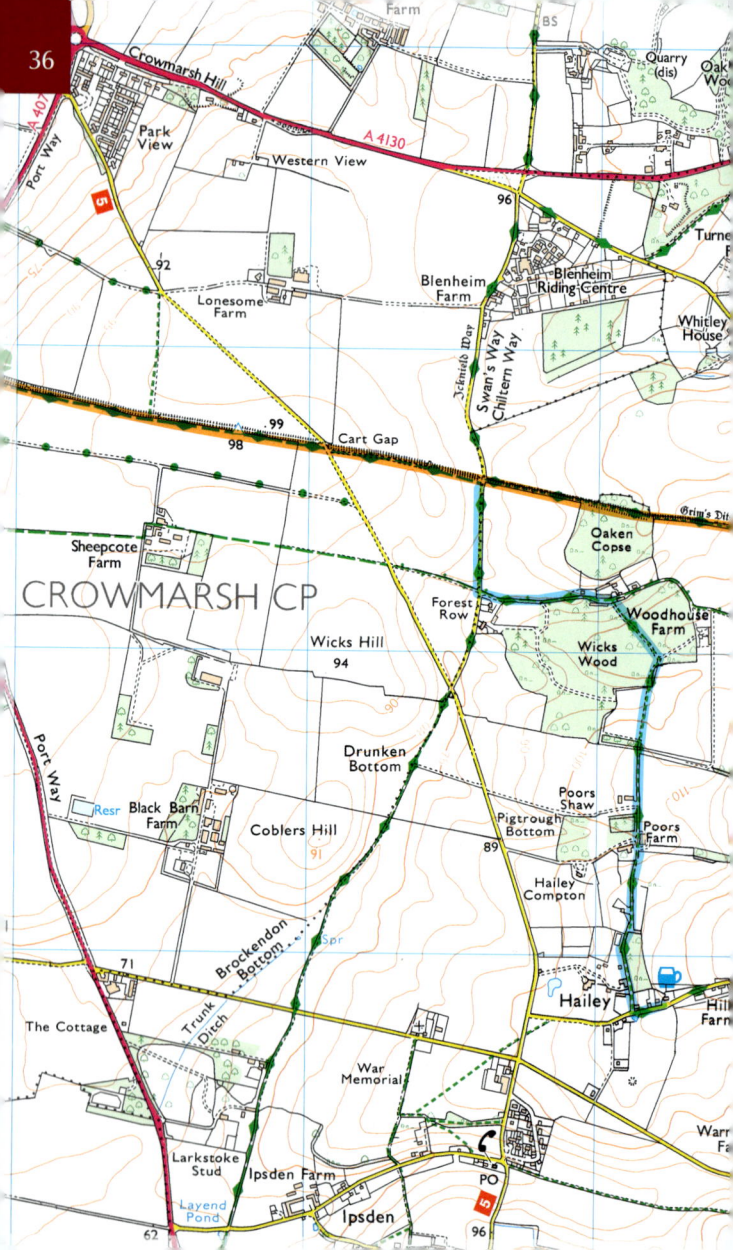

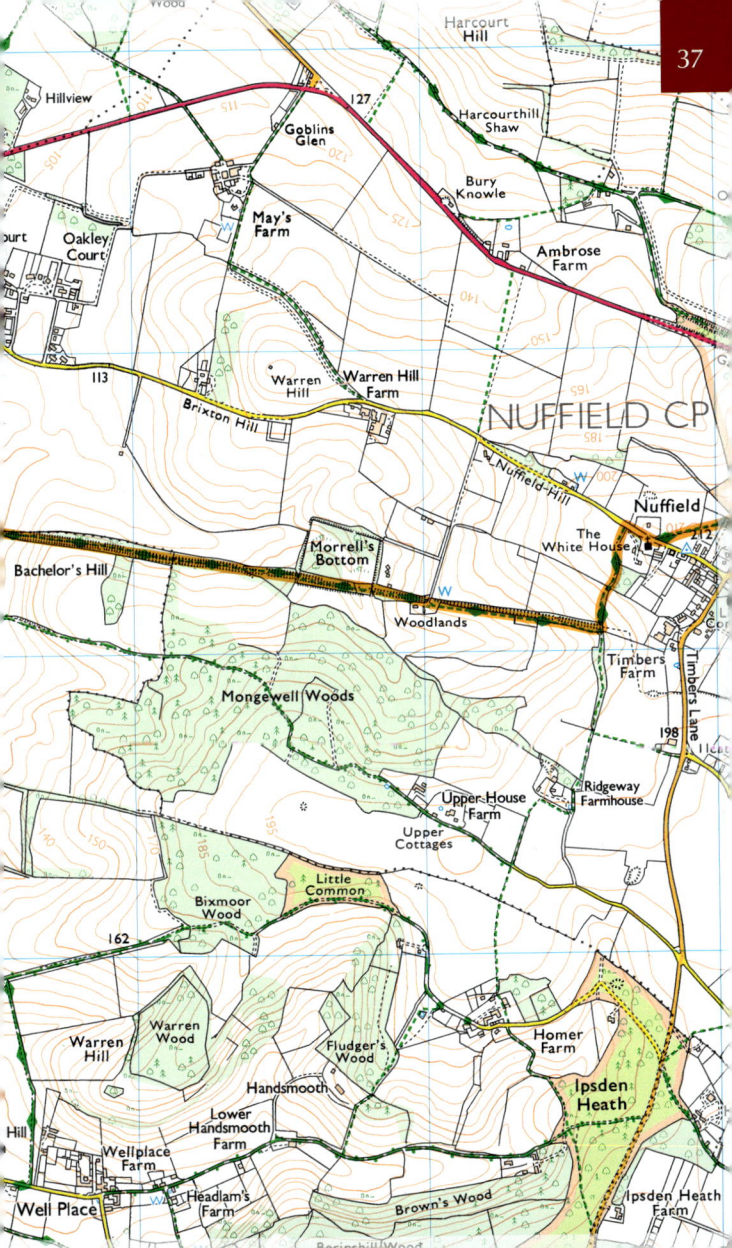

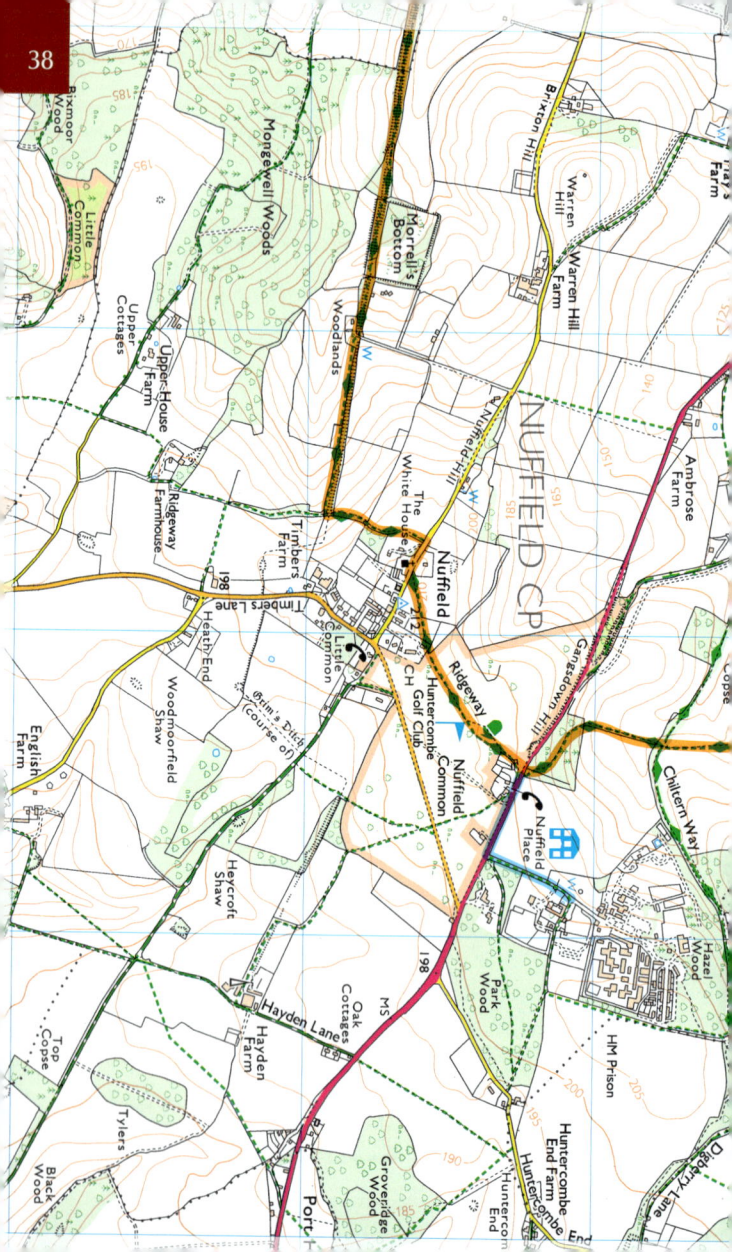

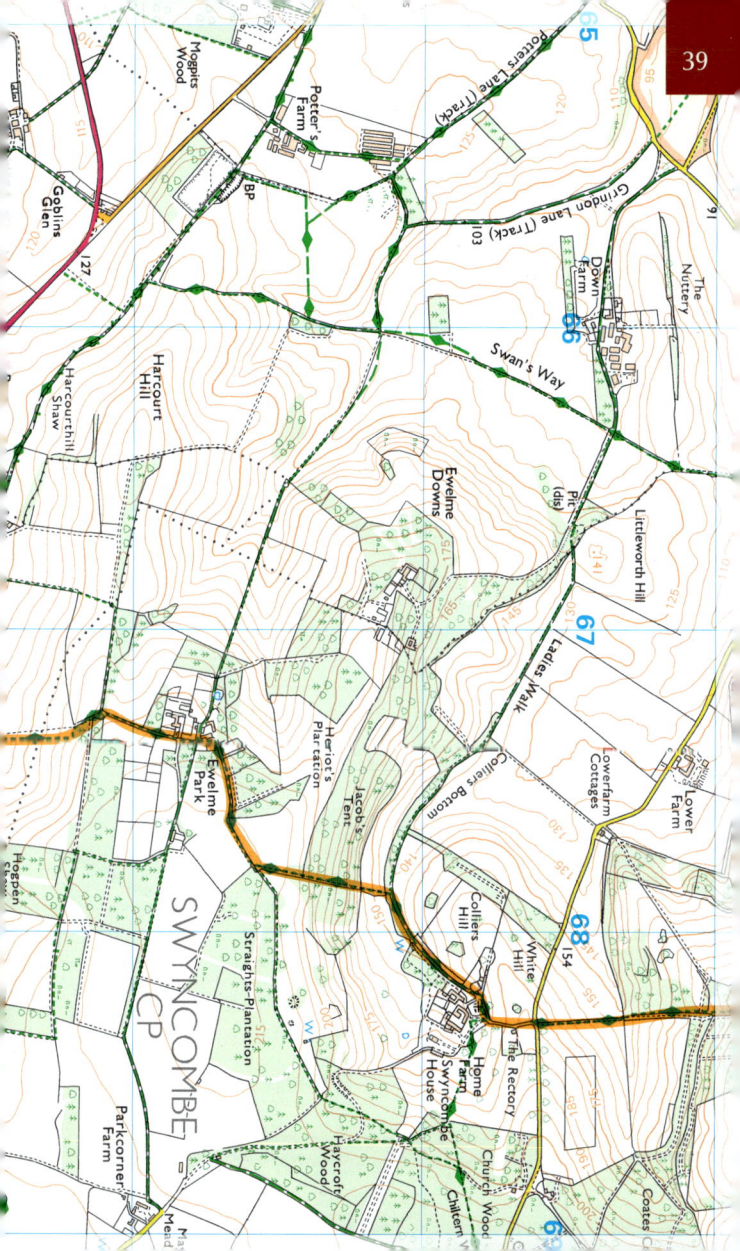

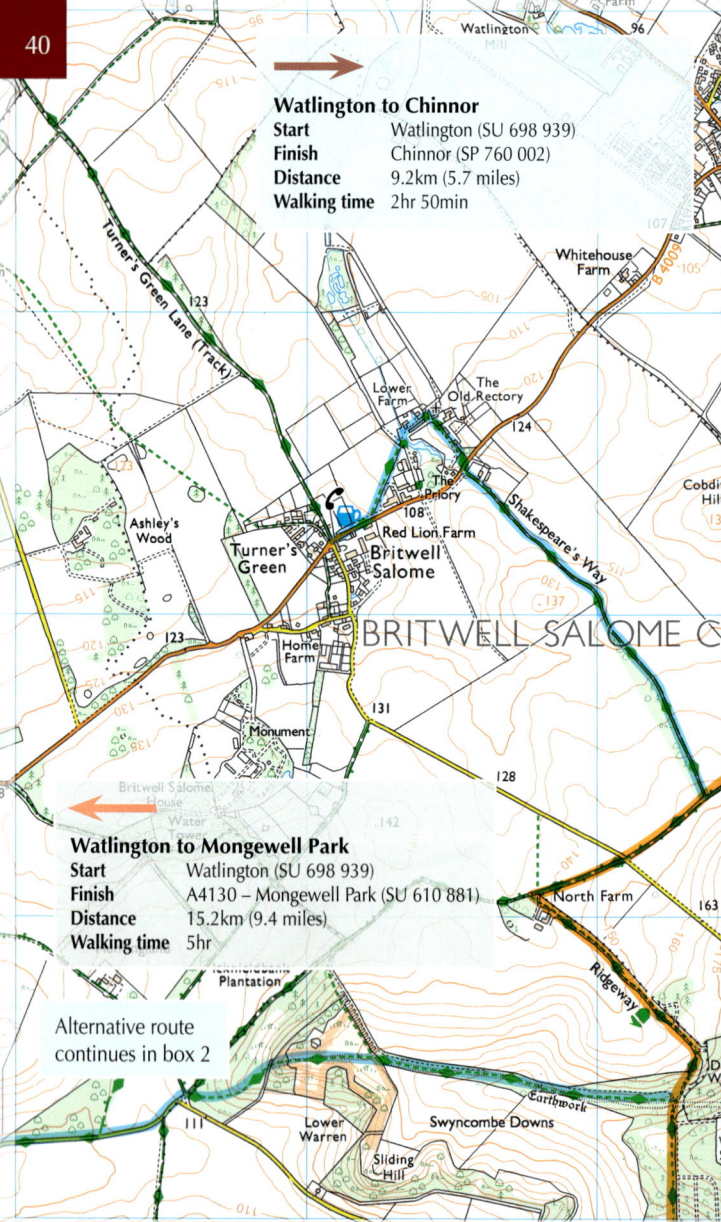

Watlington to Chinnor

Start	Watlington (SU 698 939)
Finish	Chinnor (SP 760 002)
Distance	9.2km (5.7 miles)
Walking time	2hr 50min

Watlington to Mongewell Park

Start	Watlington (SU 698 939)
Finish	A4130 – Mongewell Park (SU 610 881)
Distance	15.2km (9.4 miles)
Walking time	5hr

Alternative route
continues in box 2

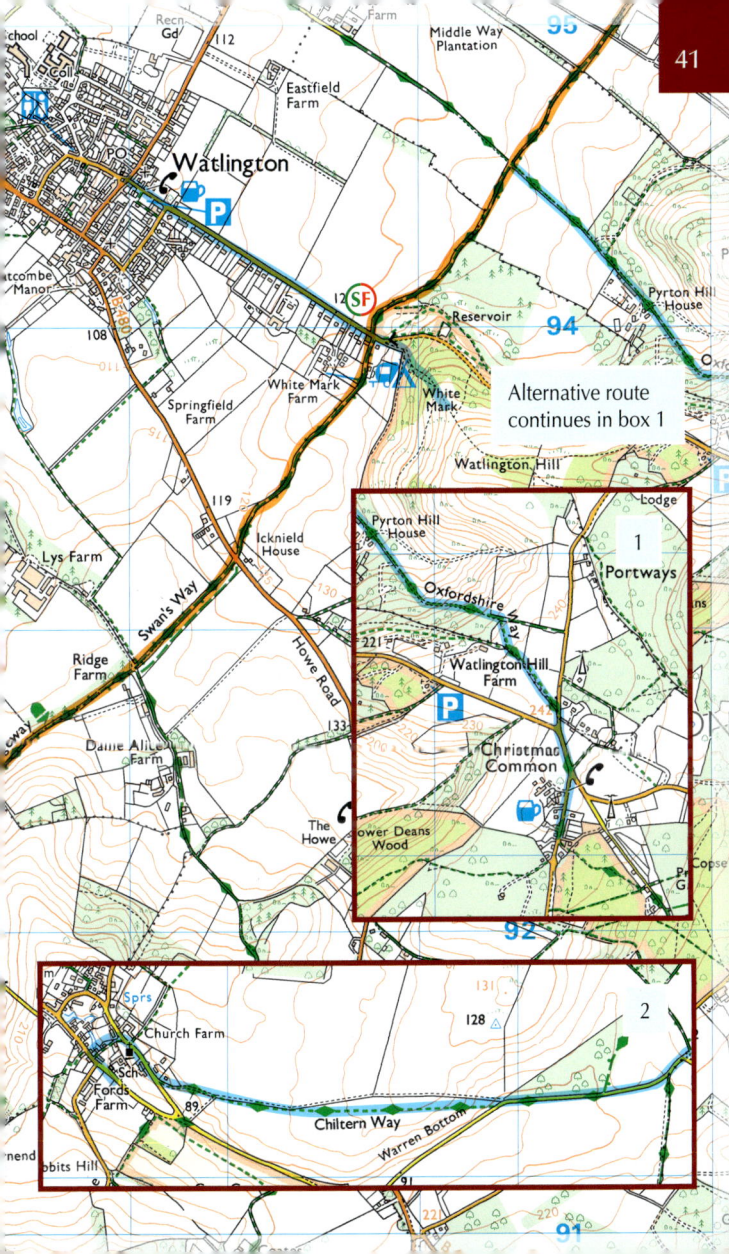

Middle Way
Plantation

95

School

Recn
Gd

112

Eastfield
Farm

Watlington

P

Pyrton Hill
House

atcombe
Manor

SF

12

Reservoir

94

Oxfo

108

110

White Mark
Farm

White
Mark

Springfield
Farm

Alternative route
continues in box 1

Watlington Hill

119

Lodge

1

Pyrton Hill
House

Portways

Lys Farm

Icknield
House

Oxfordshire Way

130

221

Watlington Hill
Farm

Swan's Way

Ridge
Farm

Howe Road

P

240

Christmas
Common

Dame Alice
Farm

133

92

The
Howe

Lower Deans
Wood

Copse
G

131

Sprs

128

2

Church Farm

Sch

Fords
Farm

89

Chiltern Way

Warren Bottom

bits Hill

nend

91

91

220

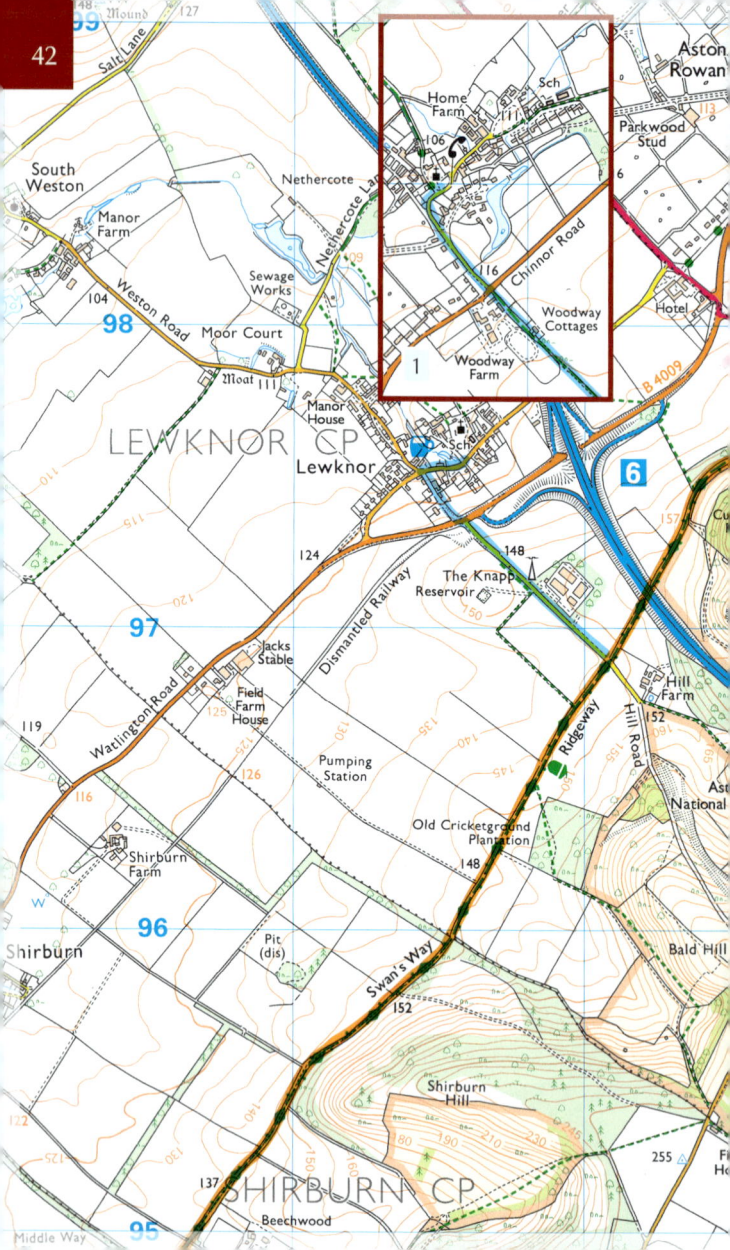

Alternative route
continues in box 1

Dismantled Railway

Race Course

Alternative route
continues in box 2

Woodway
Cottages

Woodway
Farm

116

133

Ppg
Sta

206

Kingston Wood

242

2

CP

Town
Farm

Kingston
Blount

114

Kingston
House

Gurd

144

148

201

Beacon
Hill

174

Factory

120

Dism

132

061

Little London
Wood

Radio
Station

Kiln
Farm

Dism

A 40

P

Grant's
Plantation

238

Reserve

252

North Remlets
Wood

Hailey
Wood

Chiltern Hills

Sadler's Wood

Upper Vicar's
Farm

White's
Wood

Langleygreen
Plantation

Wallace
Hill

23

P

257

Cowleaze
Wood

255

Lower Vicar's
Farm

172

Lydall's
Wood

200

172

Weston
Wood

Ibstone Road

Wellground
Farm

149

Warren

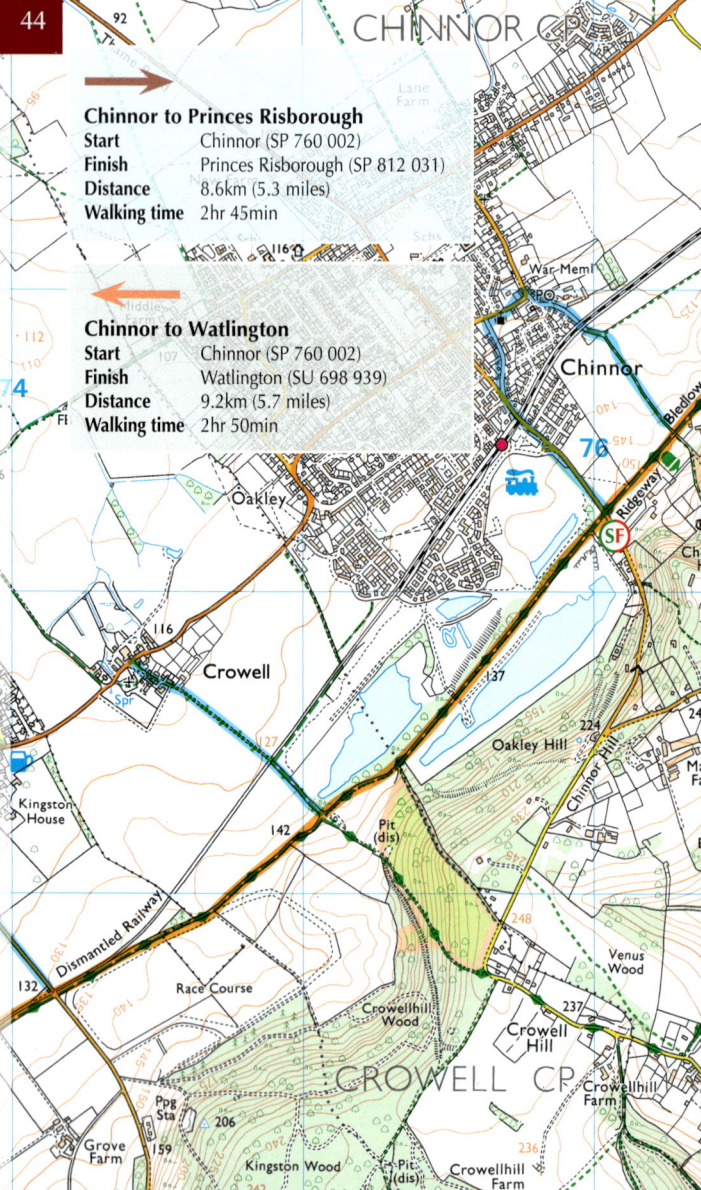

CHINNOR CP

Chinnor to Princes Risborough

Start	Chinnor (SP 760 002)
Finish	Princes Risborough (SP 812 031)
Distance	8.6km (5.3 miles)
Walking time	2hr 45min

Chinnor to Watlington

Start	Chinnor (SP 760 002)
Finish	Watlington (SU 698 939)
Distance	9.2km (5.7 miles)
Walking time	2hr 50min

Chinnor

Oakley

Crowell

Oakley Hill

Chinnor Hill

Kingston House

Pit (dis)

Dismantled Railway

Race Course

Venus Wood

Crowellhill Wood

Crowell Hill

Crowellhill Farm

CROWELL CP

Ppg Sta

Grove Farm

Kingston Wood

Pit (dis)

Crowellhill Farm

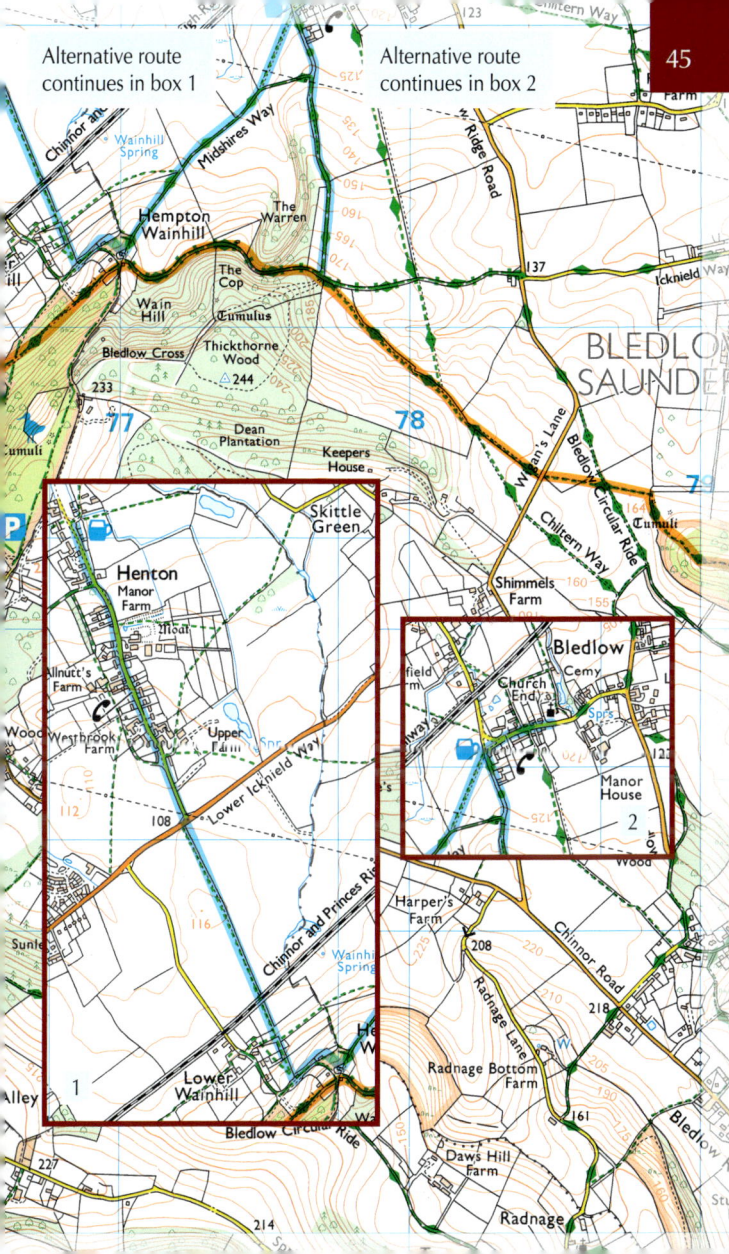

Alternative route
continues in box 1

Alternative route
continues in box 2

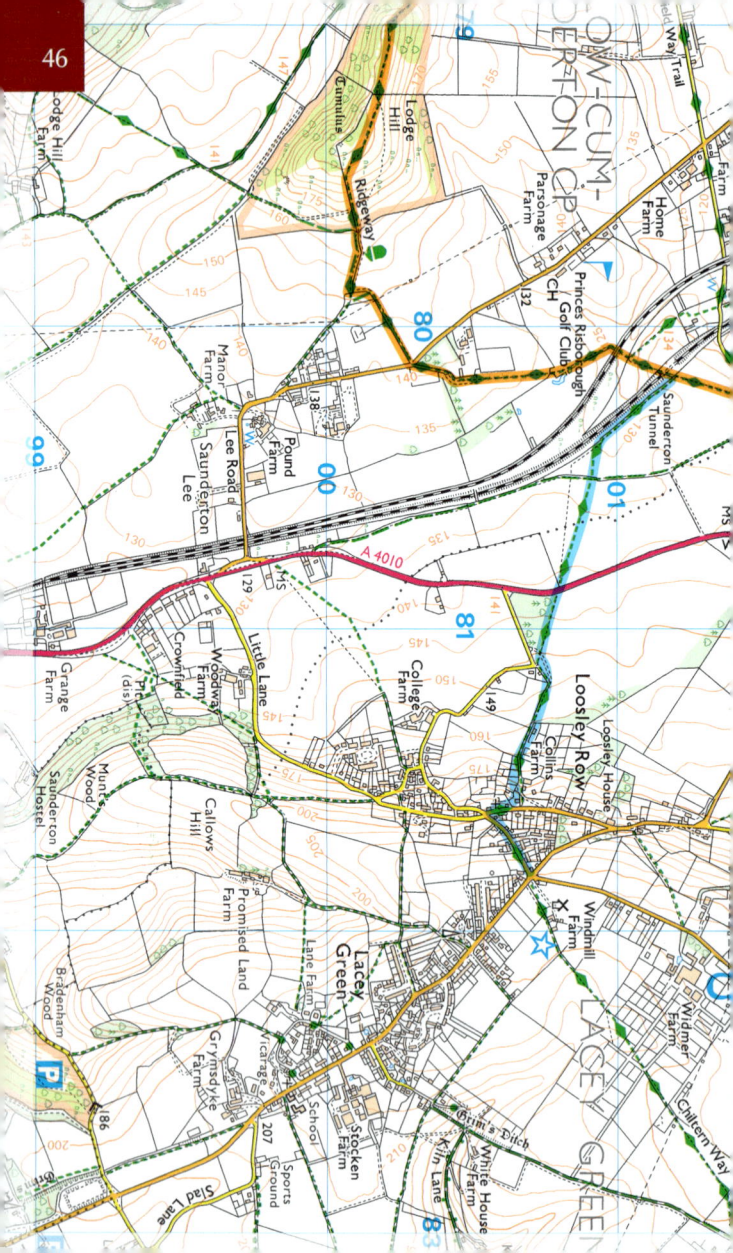

Princes Risborough to Chinnor

Start Princes Risborough (SP 812 031)

Finish Chinnor (SP 760 002)

Distance 8.6km (5.3 miles)

Walking time 2hr 45min

Princes Risborough to Wendover

Start Princes Risborough (SP 812 031)

Finish Wendover (SP 869 078)

Distance 10km (6.2 miles)

Walking time 3hr 30min

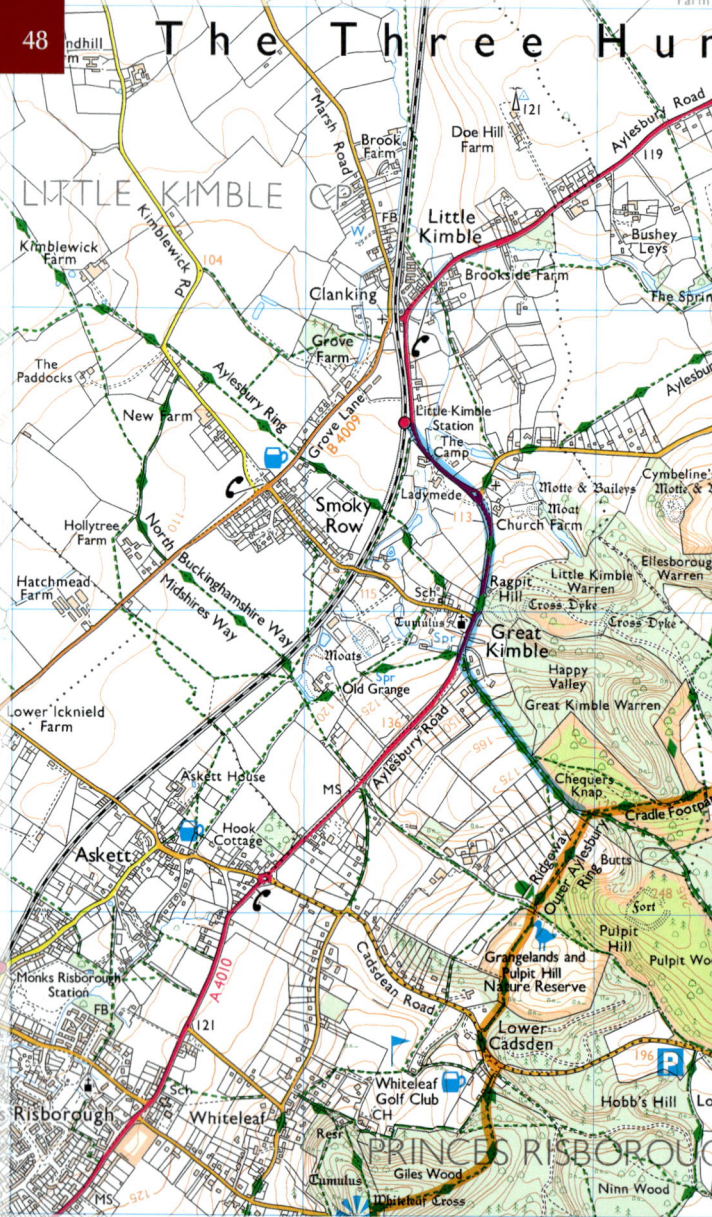

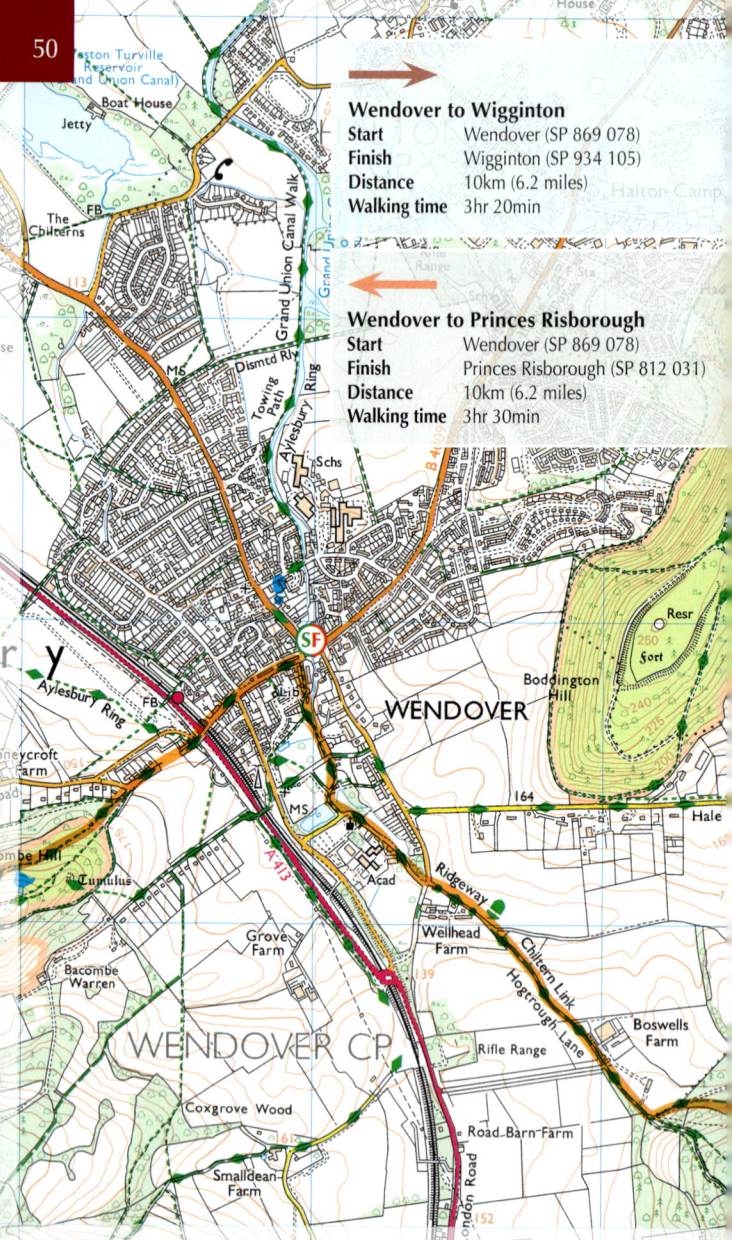

Wendover to Wigginton

Start	Wendover (SP 869 078)
Finish	Wigginton (SP 934 105)
Distance	10km (6.2 miles)
Walking time	3hr 20min

Wendover to Princes Risborough

Start	Wendover (SP 869 078)
Finish	Princes Risborough (SP 812 031)
Distance	10km (6.2 miles)
Walking time	3hr 30min

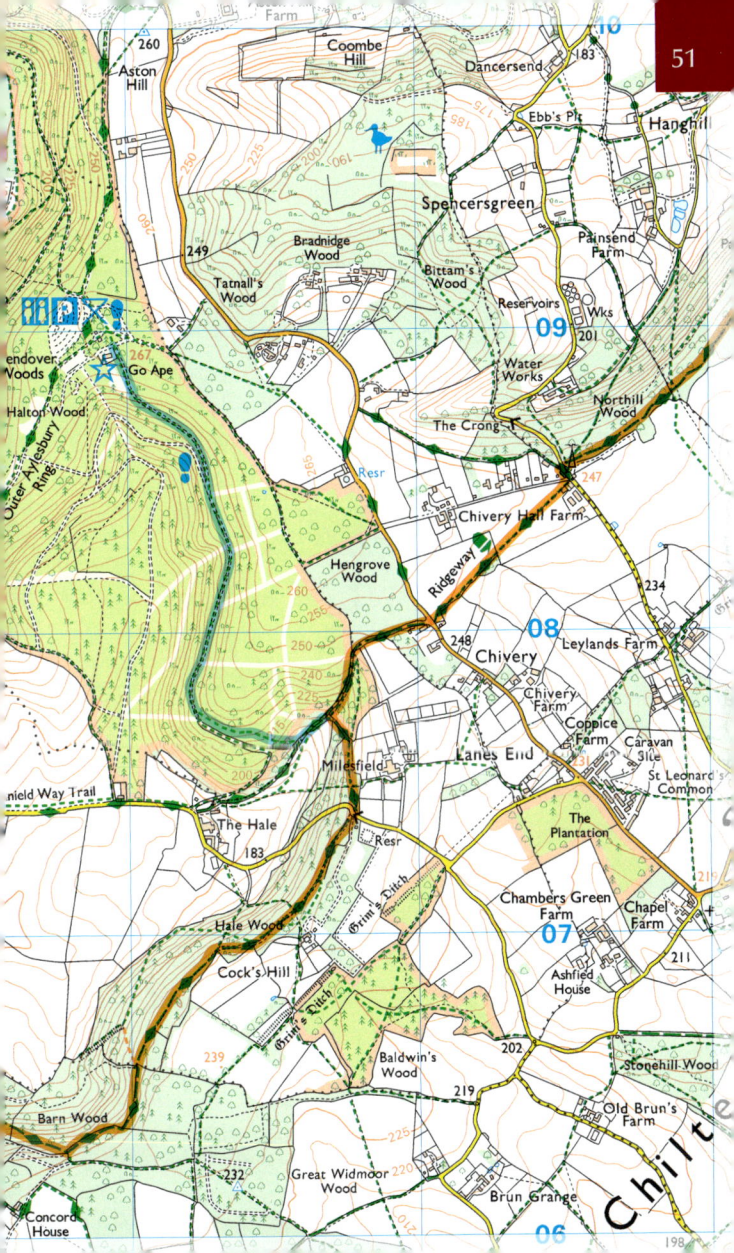

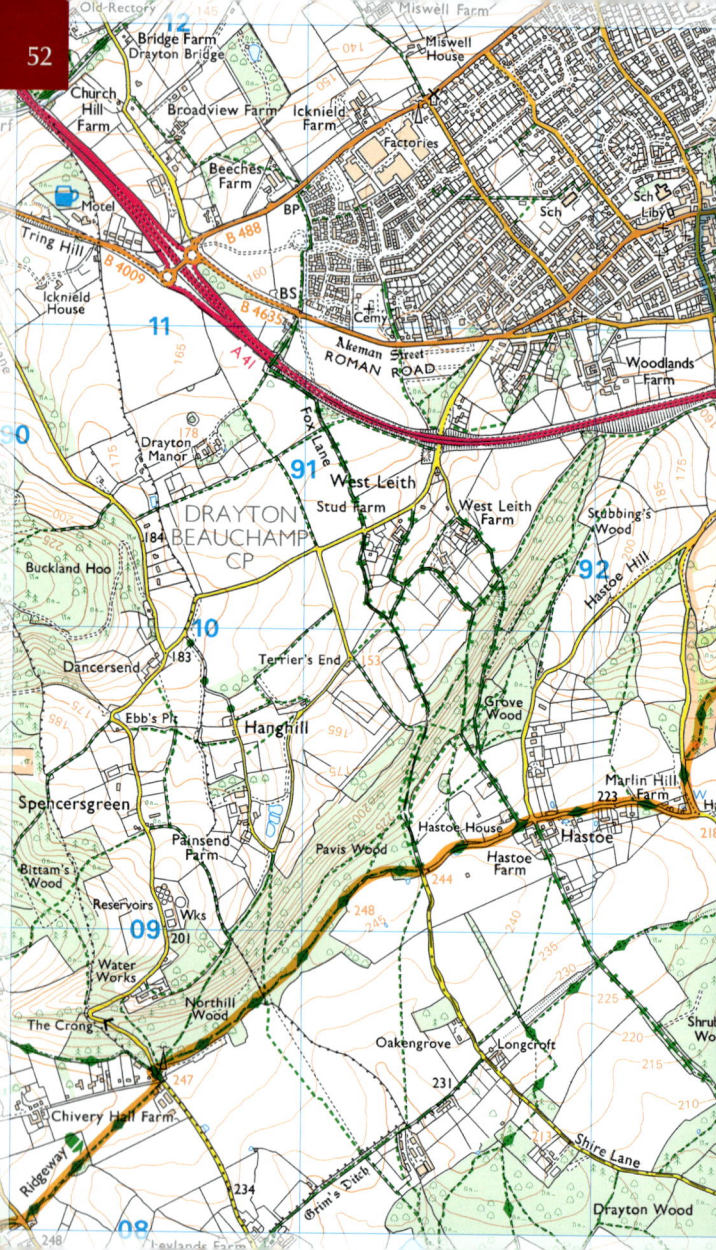

Wigginton to Ivinghoe Beacon

Start	Wigginton (SP 934 105)
Finish	Ivinghoe Beacon (SP 959 168)
Distance	8.4km (5.2 miles)
Walking time	2hr 50min

Wigginton to Wendover

Start	Wigginton (SP 934 105)
Finish	Wendover (SP 869 078)
Distance	10km (6.2 miles)
Walking time	3hr 20min

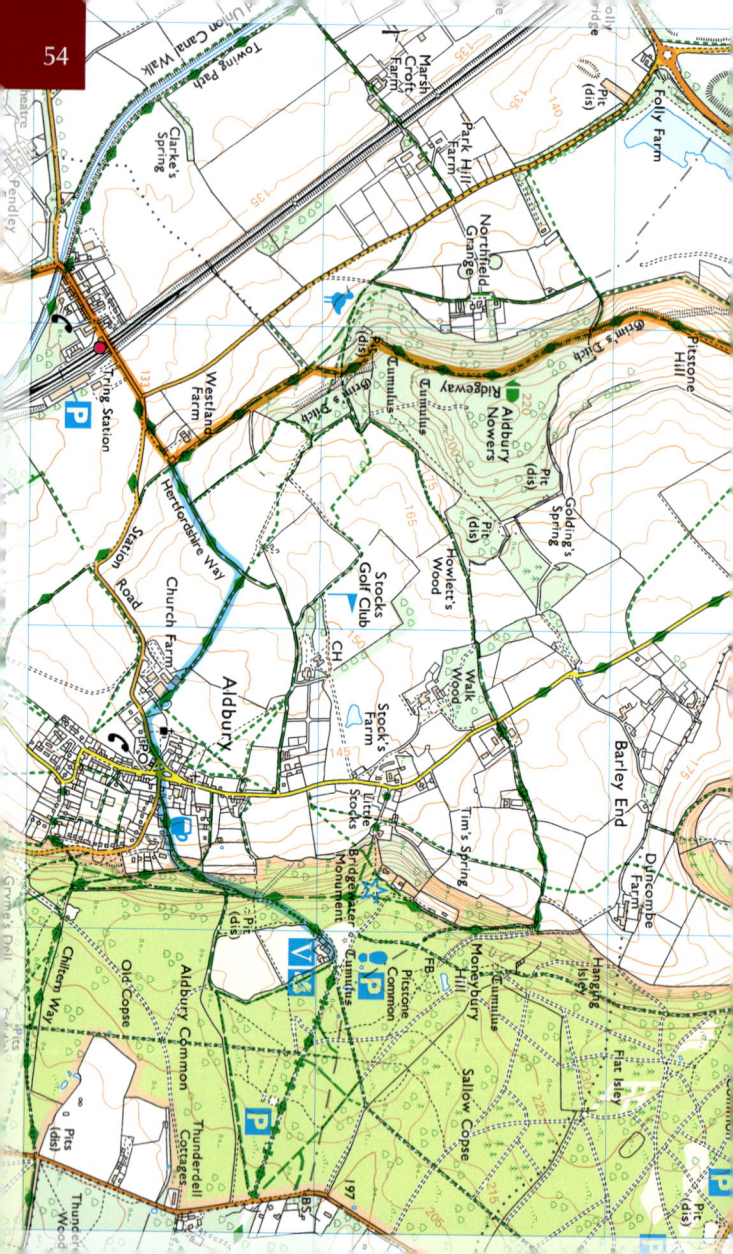

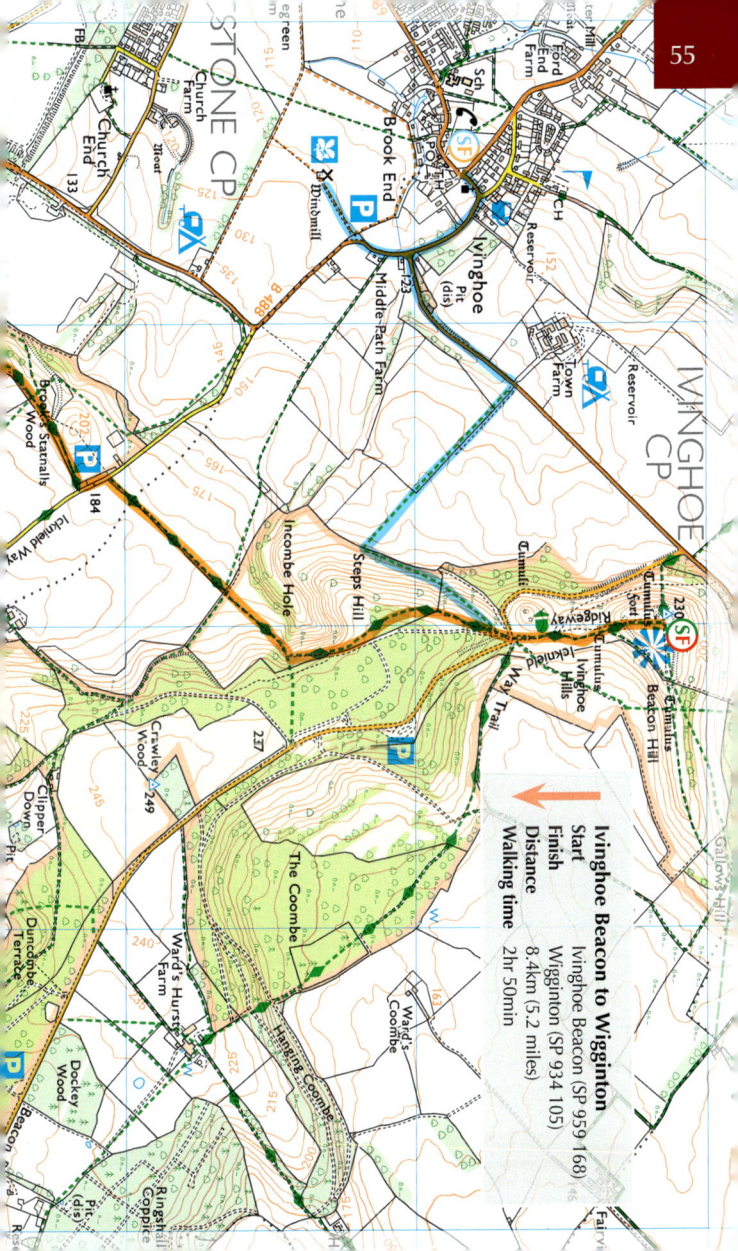

STONE CP

Church
Farm

Church
End

Brook End

Ivinghoe

Windmill

Middle Path Farm

Brook
Wood

Stathalls

Icknield Way

Incombe Hole

Steps Hill

Crawley
Wood

Clipper
Down

Pit

Duncombe
Terrace

Ward's Hurst
Farm

Dockey
Wood

Beacon

Pit
(dis)

The Coombe

Hanging Coombe

Ringshall
Coppice

Ward's
Coombe

Fairw

Gallows Hill

IVINGHOE
CP

Town
Farm

Reservoir

Reservoir

Pit
(dis)

Ivinghoe
Beacon

Ridgeway

Icknield
Way Trail

Icknield

Tumulus

Tumulus

Tumuli

Beacon Hill

Tumuli

Ivinghoe Beacon to Wigginton

Start   Ivinghoe Beacon (SP 959 168)
Finish   Wigginton (SP 934 105)
Distance   8.4km (5.2 miles)
Walking time   2hr 50min

LEGEND OF SYMBOLS
USED ON ORDNANCE SURVEY
1:25,000 (EXPLORER) MAPPING

ROADS AND PATHS — Not necessarily rights of way

M1 or A6(M)	Motorway	Service Area · Junction Number
A 35	Dual carriageway	
A30	Main road	Service Area · Toll road junction
B 3074	Secondary road	
	Narrow road with passing places	
	Road under construction	
	Road generally more than 4 m wide	
	Road generally less than 4 m wide	
	Other road, drive or track, fenced and unfenced	
	Gradient: steeper than 20% (1 in 5); 14% (1 in 7) to 20% (1 in 5)	
Ferry	Ferry; Ferry P – passenger only	
	Path	

RAILWAYS

Multiple track ⎱ standard
Single track ⎰ gauge

Narrow gauge or
Light rapid transit system
(LRTS) and station

Road over; road under; level crossing

Cutting; tunnel; embankment

Station, open to passengers; siding

PUBLIC RIGHTS OF WAY

-----------	Footpath
— — — — —	Bridleway
+ + + + +	Byway open to all traffic
— · — · — · —	Restricted byway

The representation on this map of any other road, track or path is no evidence of the existence of a right of way

ARCHAEOLOGICAL AND HISTORICAL INFORMATION

✠	Site of antiquity	VILLA	Roman	✶	Visible earthwork
⚔ 1066	Site of battle (with date)	𝕮𝖆𝖘𝖙𝖑𝖊	Non-Roman		

Information provided by English Heritage for England and the Royal Commissions on the Ancient and Historical Monuments for Scotland and Wales

OTHER PUBLIC ACCESS

• • • Other routes with public access — The exact nature of the rights on these routes and the existence of any restrictions may be checked with the local highway authority. Alignments are based on the best information available

◆ ◆ ◆ Recreational route

◆ ◆ ◆ 🚶 **National Trail**   **Long Distance Route**

– – – – – – Permissive footpath ⎫ Footpaths and bridleways along which landowners have permitted public use but which are not rights of way. The agreement may be withdrawn

– – – – Permissive bridleway ⎭

• • • Traffic-free cycle route

[1] ▮1▮ National cycle network route number – traffic free; on road

ACCESS LAND

DANGER AREA — Firing and test ranges in the area. Danger! Observe warning notices

MANAGED ACCESS — Access permitted within managed controls, for example, local byelaws. Visit **www.access.mod.uk** for information

England and Wales

 Access land boundary and tint

Access land in wooded area

 Access information point

Portrayal of access land on this map is intended as a guide to land which is normally available for access on foot, for example access land created under the Countryside and Rights of Way Act 2000, and land managed by the National Trust, Forestry Commission and Woodland Trust. Access for other activities may also exist. Some restrictions will apply; some land will be excluded from open access rights. The depiction of rights of access does not imply or express any warranty as to its accuracy or completeness. Observe local signs and follow the Countryside Code. Visit **www.countrysideaccess.gov.uk** for up-to-date information

BOUNDARIES

— + — + National

— · — · County (England)

— — — — Unitary Authority (UA), Metropolitan District (Met Dist), London Borough (LB) or District (Scotland & Wales are solely Unitary Authorities)

· · · · · · · · · Civil Parish (CP) (England) or Community (C) (Wales)

 National Park boundary

VEGETATION

Limits of vegetation are defined by positioning of symbols

🌲 🌲 Coniferous trees

Non-coniferous trees

Coppice

Orchard

Scrub

Bracken, heath or rough grassland

Marsh, reeds or saltings

HEIGHTS AND NATURAL FEATURES

52 ·	Ground survey height	Surface heights are to the nearest metre above mean sea level.
284	Air survey height	Where two heights are shown, the first height is to the base of the triangulation pillar and the second (in brackets) to the highest natural point of the hill

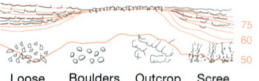

Vertical face/cliff

Loose rock · Boulders · Outcrop · Scree

Contours are at 5 or 10 metre vertical intervals

75
60
50

Water

Mud

Sand; sand and shingle

SELECTED TOURIST AND LEISURE INFORMATION

Building of historic interest		Nature reserve	
Cadw		National Trust	
Heritage centre		Other tourist feature	
Camp site		Parking	
Caravan site		Park and ride, all year	
Camping and caravan site		Park and ride, seasonal	
Castle / fort		Picnic site	
Cathedral / Abbey		Preserved railway	
Craft centre		Public Convenience	
Country park		Public house/s	
Cycle trail		Recreation / leisure / sports centre	
Mountain bike trail		Roman site (Hadrian's Wall only)	
Cycle hire		Slipway	
English Heritage		Telephone, emergency	
Fishing		Telephone, public	
Forestry Commission Visitor centre		Telephone, roadside assistance	
Garden / arboretum		Theme / pleasure park	
Golf course or links		Viewpoint	
Historic Scotland		Visitor centre	
Information centre, all year		Walks / trails	
Information centre, seasonal		World Heritage site / area	
Horse riding		Water activites	
Museum		Boat trips	
National Park Visitor Centre (park logo) e.g. Yorkshire Dales		Boat hire	

(For complete legend and symbols, see any OS Explorer map).

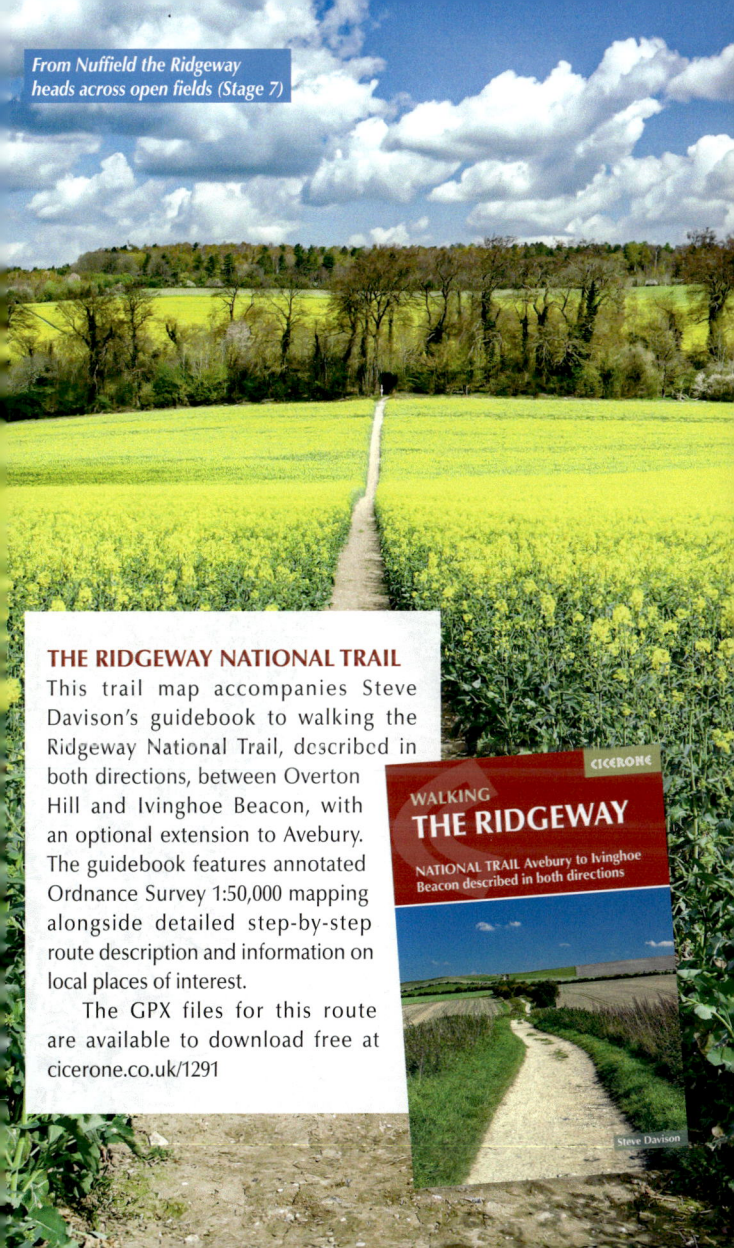

From Nuffield the Ridgeway heads across open fields (Stage 7)

THE RIDGEWAY NATIONAL TRAIL

This trail map accompanies Steve Davison's guidebook to walking the Ridgeway National Trail, described in both directions, between Overton Hill and Ivinghoe Beacon, with an optional extension to Avebury. The guidebook features annotated Ordnance Survey 1:50,000 mapping alongside detailed step-by-step route description and information on local places of interest.

The GPX files for this route are available to download free at cicerone.co.uk/1291

CICERONE

WALKING
THE RIDGEWAY

NATIONAL TRAIL Avebury to Ivinghoe
Beacon described in both directions

Steve Davison

Cicerone's gold-standard guides, now digital

Expert-curated routes

Follow routes crafted by expert authors who know each area inside out.

Plan with confidence

Find detailed facilities information and discover local landmarks along the way.

Download GPS-enabled maps

Navigate confidently wherever you are, even without a signal.

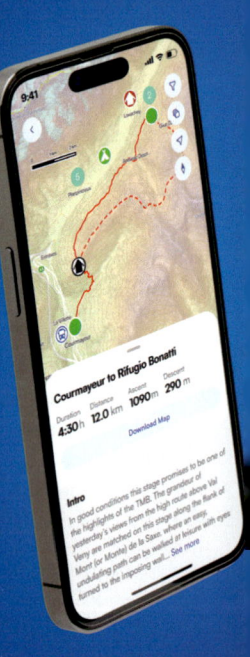

Discover more adventures in our expanding collection at

cicerone.co.uk